11-00X

Food
Standar
Agency
food.gov.u

D1765579

FOOL
PORTION
SIZES

Third Edition

London: TSO

Published for the Food Standards Agency under licence from the Controller of Her Majesty's Stationery Office.

© Crown Copyright 1988

First published 1988
Second edition 1993
Third edition 2002
Tenth impression 2010

ISBN 978 0 11 242961 6

INTRODUCTION

This book has been compiled primarily by Alison Mills and Sejal Patel and continues the concept of the first edition by Helen Crawley.

As before this book provides up to date information on typical weights and portion sizes of foods eaten in Britain. It provides dietitians, nutritionists, and anyone wishing to estimate how much they eat, with average values for the weights of both individual food items and average portion sizes. By using this book in conjunction with nutritional information on food labels or a standard reference book of food composition such as the Food Standards Agency's Manual of Nutrition, McCance and Widdowson's 'The Composition of Foods'[1] and its supplements (all of which present nutrient value in 100g of the food), the energy and nutrients in portions of the foods and therefore in a typical day's meals can be calculated.

This edition now includes information that has been collected during a large number of recent weighed dietary studies carefully conducted by the Ministry of Agriculture, Fisheries and Food throughout Britain. In addition a large number of weights have been revised from manufacturers' information and by weighing numerous new items of food, particularly take-away foods and some foods which are not yet required by law to be labelled with their weight.

The weights in this book fall into two categories:

1 Weights of specific discrete items, e.g. a packet of crisps, a chocolate bar, a biscuit, an ice-lolly etc.
2 Average portions of larger items, e.g. of pasta, vegetables, apple crumble etc.

Individual items

In many cases a specific name or brand is sufficient to distinguish a particular product e.g. a 'bourbon biscuit', but it is still important to check the weight given on the packet wherever possible. Weights of manufactured foods may vary as manufacturers increase and decrease weights and prices, or may offer larger packs for promotional purchases. It is important to be aware that all 'standard' weights can vary from those printed here and that there can be significant differences between brands.

Portion sizes indicated in this book are not necessarily intended to relate to serving sizes for the purposes of nutrition claims, these being subject to special legal provisions in their own right.

Where the information is less specific this book can also be used to obtain a suitable estimate or average value. In such cases, first check the exact food description: an apple can be 'small' or 'large', and other foods as purchased can vary from the 'bite size' to the 'economy'. If the packet is not available, an idea of size or purchase price, number of items in a pack or outlet from which it was purchased can all provide useful information. We have tried to include as far as possible the main variations in weight for the same food.

Average portion sizes

Portions from larger items or packets are more variable and this book can at best only provide an estimate of the actual amount consumed. Whilst the values should be reasonably accurate across a population, any individual's intake could be quite different. For example, a child's portion could be smaller and an active man's portion could be larger. However, many weights can be made more accurate if more is known about the food eaten, eg half a large tin of baked beans or a small bowl of cornflakes. Users may need to weigh particular foods to familiarise themselves with small, medium and large portions or thick and thin spreadings. It is often more difficult to assign portion sizes to food eaten outside the home but weights of many standard fast foods and ethnic dishes have been included in the appropriate section.

The book is divided into sections alphabetically, and foods are then listed alphabetically within each group. Foods which fit into more than one section may appear twice. There will also inevitably be cases where regional or ethnic dishes appear under names other than the familiar local names.

This is the second edition of what is planned to be a regularly updated book, and we would appreciate users' and manufacturers' comments on presentation and on specific weights. We would also welcome suggestions for extending it further.

We would like to thank Alison Blackburn, Sarah Darbyshire, Susan Lee and Gillian Smithers of Nutrition Branch I, for their help and advice in compiling the information in this book.

We would also like to thank the following manufacturers who provided information for the revision of this book:

Birds Eye Wall's Limited, The Biscuit Cake Chocolate and Confectionery Alliance, The Boots Company PLC, Burger King UK Ltd, Cadbury Ltd, Colman's of Norwich, The Federation of Bakers, The Food and Drink Federation, H J Heinz Company Limited, Kelloggs, Kentucky Fried Chicken GB Ltd, Lyons Bakeries (UK Ltd), Mars Confectionery, McDonald's Restaurants Limited, McVities (UK), Meat and Livestock Commission, Milupa, Nestlé UK Ltd, Nestlé Rowntree, Pizzaland International Ltd, Red Mill Snack Foods Ltd, RHM Food Limited, Snack Nut and Crisp Manufacturers Association Ltd, St Ivel Ltd and Wimpy International.

Nutrition Branch I
Ministry of Agriculture,
Fisheries and Food
1993

[1] McCance and Widdowson's 'The Composition of Foods'. 5th Edition B Holland, A A Welch, I D Unwin, D H Buss, A A Paul and D A T Southgate. The Royal Society of Chemistry, 1991.

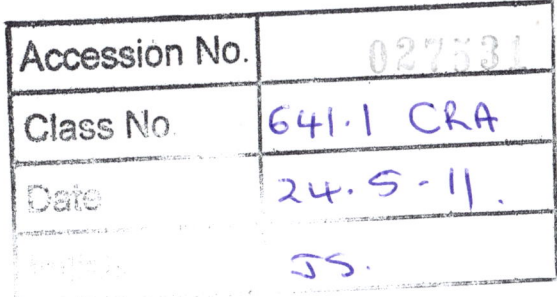

CONTENTS

Standard weights and measures

1 ounce	=	28.35g
1 pound	=	453.6g
1 gram	=	0.0353oz
1 kilogram	=	2.20516lb

1 fluid ounce	=	28.41ml
1 pint	=	568.3ml
1 litre	=	1.76 pints

1 teaspoonful	=	$\frac{1}{8}$ fl oz	=	about 5ml
1 dessertspoonful	=	$\frac{1}{4}$ fl oz	=	about 10ml
1 tablespoonful	=	$\frac{1}{2}$ fl oz	=	about 15ml

SPECIFIC GRAVITIES OF COMMONLY CONSUMED FOODS

All typical portion sizes presented in this book are given in grams of the edible portion of the food unless otherwise stated. Since many dairy products and beverages may be sold or measured by volume, typical specific gravities (densities) of some of these products are given in the table below. To convert volumes into grams multiply by the appropriate specific gravity.

Food and drink	Specific gravity
Milk products and eggs	
Skimmed milk	1.036
Semi-skimmed milk	1.034
Whole milk	1.031
Condensed milk (sweetened)	1.160
Evaporated milk (unsweetened)	1.066
Single cream	1.000
Whipping cream	0.990
Double cream	0.990
Yoghurts	1.080
	(range 1.030–1.200)
Ice cream	variable 0.500–0.600
Eggs	1.020

Food and drink	Specific gravity
Fats and oils	
Palm oil	0.890
Other vegetable oils	0.910–0.925
Selected beverages	
Baby drinks	
Baby fruit juice	1.040
Baby fruit juice drink, concentrated	1.320
Carbonated drinks, not low calorie	
Barley crush	1.070
Cola	1.040
Fruit juice drink	1.040
Lemonade	1.020
Concentrated fruit drinks, not low calorie	
Any fruit not blackcurrant	1.100
Barley water, any fruit, not blackcurrant	1.100
Mixed fruit	variable 1.09–1.120
Ribena—blackcurrant	1.280
Concentrated fruit drinks, low calorie	
Citrus	1.030
Mixed fruit	1.010
Fruit juice	1.020
Fruit juice drinks, ready to drink, not low calorie	
Apple flavour	1.040
Citrus	1.040
Mixed fruit	1.030
Ribena—blackcurrant	1.050

Food and drink	Specific gravity
Fruit drinks, not low calorie	
Mixed fruit with blackcurrant	1.040
Mixed fruit not blackcurrant	1.030
Fruit drinks, low calorie	
Mixed fruit not blackcurrant	1.010
High juice, not blackcurrant, not low calorie	
Concentrated	1.150
Ready to drink	1.040
Milk drinks	
Drink, skimmed milk with whole milk, chocolate flavoured	1.050
Drink, skimmed milk with whole milk, not chocolate flavoured	1.040
Mars milk	1.070
Cadbury's skimmed milk based, milk chocolate drink	1.060
Milk shake, whole milk based, UHT, purchased	1.060
Yoghurt drink containing puréed fruit	1.060
Alcoholic beverages	
Beers	
Beer, bitter, canned	1.008
Beer, bitter, low alcohol	1.020
Beer, draught	1.004
Beer, keg	1.001
Beer, mild draught	1.009
Brown ale, bottled	1.008
Lager, bottled	1.005
Lager, low alcohol	1.010

Food and drink	Specific gravity
Lager, alcohol-free	1.010
Pale ale, bottled	1.003
Stout, bottled	1.014
Stout, extra	1.002
Strong ale	1.018
Ciders	
Cider, dry	1.007
Cider, sweet	1.012
Cider, vintage	1.017
Cider, low alcohol	1.020
Wines	
Red wine	0.998
Rose wine, medium	1.003
White wine, dry	0.995
White wine, medium	1.005
White wine, sparkling	0.995
White wine, sweet	1.016
Fortified wines	
Port	1.026
Sherry, dry	0.988
Sherry, medium	0.988
Sherry, sweet	1.009
Vermouths	
Vermouth, dry	1.005
Vermouth, sweet	1.046
Liqueurs	
Advocaat	1.093

Food and drink	Specific gravity
Cherry brandy	1.093
Curaçao	1.052
Spirits	
40% volume	0.950

BABY FOODS

Boots, First Harvest	Dessert starter	*125g*
	Infant desserts	*125g*
	Infant savouries, from 4 months	*125g*
	Junior desserts	*190g*
	Junior savouries, from 7 months	*190g*
	Savoury starters, from 3 months	*125g*
Cow and Gate	Ready to drink baby juice (125mls)	*130g*
	Stage 1 jars	*150g*
	Stage 2 jars	*200g*
Dried/powdered baby foods	1 average tablespoon	*5g*
Fromage frais	Baby Danone	*60g*
	Heinz, jar	*150g*
Heinz	Desserts, from 3 months, can	*128g*
	jar	*163g*
	Savoury dishes, from 3 months, can	*128g*
	jar	*128g*
	Savoury dishes, from 7 months, can	*163g*
	standard jar	*163g*
	large jar	*200g*
Milupa	Baby Rice Flakes, 1 tablespoon	*5g*
	Fine Oat Flakes, 1 tablespoon	*2.5g*
	Infant Foods, 1 tablespoon	*5g*
	Junior Foods, 1 tablespoon	*5g*
	Junior Drink, 1 heaped teaspoon	*3.8g*
	Sugarfree Fennel Infant Drink, 1 scoop	*0.3g*
	Wholewheat Flakes, 1 tablespoon	*5g*
Robinson's	Ready to drink baby juice (250mls)	*260g*
Rusks	Boots, Original	*6g*
	Ruskmen	*8g*
	Low sugar, flavoured	*10g*
	Farley's original	*17g*
	Liga	*8g*

Yoghurts (baby)	Cow & Gate, jar	*150g*
	Heinz yoghurt dessert, jar	*150g*
	St Ivel Baby & Toddler	*90g*

BEVERAGES

Refer to pp viii–xii to convert volumes to grams.

Alcoholic drinks

Babycham	1 bottle	*100g*
Barley wine	1 bottle	*180g*
Beer/lager	1 pint	*574g*
	½ pint	*287g*
	bottle	*250/300g*
	small can	*333g*
	large can	*444g*
Liqueurs	1 measure	*25g*
Sherry	1 glass, small	*50g*
	large	*100g*
Spirits	1 measure (England and Wales)	*23g*
	(Scotland)	*27g*
	(N. Ireland)	*35g*
	1 airline measure	*48g*
	1 miniature	*29g*
Vermouth	1 measure	*48g*
Wine	1 average glass	*125g*
	1 small bottle	*200g*
	1 half bottle	*375g*
	1 average bottle	*750g*

Soft drinks and fruit juices

Many beverages are sold or measured by volume.
To convert into grams multiply by the appropriate specific gravity. (see table pp viii–xii).

Carbonated bottled drink	Lucozade (glass bottle)	*250ml*
	Own brand (plastic bottle)—large	*500ml*
	Own brand (plastic bottle)—standard	*250ml*

Carbonated canned drink	slim can	*250ml*
	sports/large can	*500ml*
	standard can	*330ml*
	trial/funsize/baby can	*150ml*
Cup drinks	Calypso	*191g*
	Scotts	*191g*
Dilutable still drinks	average measure	*50g*
Fresh orange juice	1 orange, freshly squeezed	*50g*
Fruit Juice	average glass	*160g*
	individual carton	*200g*
	tall tumbler	*300g*
	wine glass	*120g*
	Britvic canned	*173g*
	pub bottle	*110g*
Lime cordial	in ½ pint lager	*45g*
	in 1 pint lager	*90g*
Mineral water	large	*500g*
	standard	*330g*
	small	*250g*
	Evian, small	*200g*
	canned, standard	*330g*
	canned, small	*250g*
Mixers	pub bottle	*110g*
	Schweppes, bottled	*250ml*
	standard, bottle	*330ml*
	tonic water, canned	*170ml*
Pouch drinks	Capri Sun	*208g*
	Geebee Twist & Squeeze	*201g*
	Lucozade Sport Isotonic drink	*250g*
	Luvly Jubbly pouch drink	*206g*

Ready to drink still fruit drinks

These are generally purchased in 200ml or 250ml cartons. Some examples of common types:

200ml cartons	Del Monte Fruit Troop	*206g*
	Five Alive fruit juice drinks	*206g*
	Libby's C drinks	*208g*
	Libby's Um Bongo	*206g*
	Suncrest fruit drinks	*206g*
250ml cartons	C-Vit	*263g*
	Own brand, fruit drinks	*257g*
	Own brand, fruit juice drinks	*257g*
	Own brand, Hi juice drinks	*260g*
	Quosh fruit drink	*257g*
	Robinson's Special 'R' fruit juice drinks	*253g*
	Rowntree fruit juice drink	*257g*
	Wells Sugar free fruit drinks	*253g*
Ribena	concentrate, average measure	*38g*
	individual carton	*263g*
	kingsize carton	*394g*
Squash (concentrate)	average measure	*50g*
	diluted (1:4)	*250g*

Other beverages

Cadbury's highlights	1 sachet	*11g*
Chocolate break	1 sachet	*28g*
Chocolate drinks, instant	1 sachet, average	*11g*
Chococino (Nestlé)	1 sachet	*20g*
Cocoa	1 teaspoon heaped	*6g*
	level	*2g*
Coffee	1 average cup	*190g*
	1 average mug	*260g*
	1 average vending machine cup	*170g*
	1 teaspoon instant, heaped	*2g*
	level	*1g*

Cappucino (Nescafé)	1 sachet	*13g*
unsweetened	1 sachet	*12g*
Drinking chocolate	for 1 mug	*18g*
Horlicks chocolate malted food drink	for 1 mug	*20g*
Horlicks, instant, low fat	1 sachet	*32g*
Horlicks malted food drink	for 1 mug	*25g*
	1 sachet	*23g*
Lemon tea, instant	1 teaspoon	*2g*
	for 1 mug	*6g*
Nesquik	for 1 tumbler of milk	*15g*
	1 rounded teaspoon	*5g*
Ovaltine	for 1 mug	*20g*
	1 sachet	*23g*
Ovaltine light	1 sachet	*20g*
Tea	1 average cup	*190g*
	1 average mug	*260g*
	1 average vending machine cup	*170g*

BISCUITS

Abbey Crunch		*9g*
All butter shortbread, McVities		*20g*
All butter thins		*5g*
Animals		*10g*
Arrowroot, thin		*8g*
Assorted creams		*12g*
Bandit		*24g*
Bath Oliver		*15g*
Blue Ribband	standard	*22g*
	mini	*12g*
Boasters, McVities	double chocolate	*19g*
	hazlenut/pecan	*17g*
Bourbon		*13g*
Brandy snaps		*15g*
Breakaway		*24g*
Butter crunch		*7g*
Butter puffs		*10g*
Caramel wafer, Tunnocks		*27g*
Carr's Table Water	large	*8g*
	small	*3g*
	with sesame seeds	*3g*
Cereal bars, Boots		*30g*
Cheddars		*4g*
Mini Cheddars	bag	*33g*
	each	*2g*
Cheese sandwich		*7g*
Cheese thins		*4g*
Chocolate and nut cookies		*8g*
Chocolate chip gingers		*13g*
Chocolate chip oaties		*7g*
Chocolate coated ginger and pear bar, Boots		*45g*
Chocolate fingers		*6g*
Classic bar, Fox's		*34g*
Club	(all except wafer)	*24g*
Club wafer		*19g*
Cluster	(all varieties)	*28g*

Coconut cookies		*15g*
Coconut mallows		*11g*
Cookies, Boots		*17g*
Mini cookies	per bag	*30g*
	Boots, per bag	*40g*
Corn crisp	⅛	*20g*
Cream crackers		*7g*
Crispbread	crackerbread	*10g*
	extra thin	*5g*
	Kavli, muesli	*10g*
	Ryvita	*10g*
	Scanda	*6g*
	wholewheat	*15g*
Crunchy bars, Jordans		*33g*
Custard creams		*11g*

Digestive		
	chocolate bar, McVities	*19g*
	chocolate, McVities	*18g*
	creams, McVities	*14g*
	full coated	*20g*
	McVities	*15g*
	sweetmeal	*13g*
	sweet meal, chocolate	*13g*

Farleys rusk		*17g*
Farmhouse crackers		*8g*
Fig rolls		*15g*
Fingers, chocolate coated		*6g*
54321		*21g*
Fivers		*17g*
Flapjacks	Boots	*70g*
	Large	*90g*
	Yoghurt coated	*50g*
French toast		*8g*
Fruit shortcake		*10g*
Fruit Shrewsbury		*15g*

Garibaldi		*10g*
Giant cookies	Boots, Paterson Bronté	*60g*
	Own brand	*50g*
Ginger bar, McVities	chocolate coated	*28g*

Ginger crunch creams		*13g*
Ginger nuts		*10g*
Ginger snaps		*7g*
Ginger thins		*7g*
Gipsy creams		*13g*
Gold bar		*22g*
Golden crumble		*9g*
Golden crunch creams		*13g*
Harvest crunch bars		*20g*
Hi-Lo crackers		*5g*
Hob-nob bar		*27g*
Hob-nobs	chocolate coated	*16g*
	creams	*14g*
	plain	*14g*
Hovis crackers		*7g*
Iced gems	per bag	*30g*
	each	*2g*
Iced ring biscuits		*12g*
Iced shorties		*9g*
Jaffa cakes		*13g*
Jam rings		*13g*
Jam sandwich creams		*13g*
Jamboree mallow		*20g*
Jammy dodgers		*17g*
Jaspers		*13g*
	chocolate coated	*15g*
Jump cereal bar		*21g*
Kavli	muesli crispbread	*10g*
Kracka wheat		*7g*
Krisprolls		*10g*
Lemon puffs		*10g*
Lincoln biscuits		*8g*
Mallows		*17g*
Malted milk		*9g*
Malted milk creams		*12g*
Marie		*8g*

Biscuits

Marshmallow teacake		*18g*
Maryland cookies		*9g*
Mini cookies	Boots, bag	*40g*
	McVities, bag	*30g*
	each	*3g*
Misbits		*10g*
Montana		*29g*
Morning coffee		*5g*
Munchmallow		*18g*

Nice	finger	*5g*

Oatcakes	round	*13g*
	triangle	*17g*
Orange creams		*12g*
Original crunchy bars,		
Jordans		*33g*

Peanut sticks	bag	*30g*
Penguin		*25g*
Petit beurre		*7g*
Petticoat tails		*13g*
Plain chocolate digestive	sweetmeal	*13g*
Plain chocolate homewheat	McVities	*17g*

Raisin and honey, Prewetts		*15g*
Rice cake		*7g*
Rich tea		*7g*
	chocolate coated	*13g*
Ritz	cheese sandwich	*8g*
	plain	*3g*
Riva, McVities	2 piece bar	*25g*
Rocky biscuit		*29g*
Ryvita		*10g*

Sesame seed thins	crackers	*4g*
Shortbread finger		*13g*
Shortcake		*10g*
Snack, Cadbury's		*5g*
Snowballs		*25g*

Taxi		*14g*

Tetley tea folk		*24g*
Thin arrowroot		*8g*
Toffypops		*18g*
Tracker	standard	*37g*
	packet of 6, each	*27g*
	buttermunch	*18g*
Treacle crunch creams		*13g*
Trio		*24g*
Triple bar		*22g*
Tuc	each	*5g*
	savoury sandwich	*14g*
Tuc, mini	bag	*25g*
	each	*2g*
Twiglets	standard	*50g*
	packet of 6, each	*25g*
	each	*1g*
Typhoo Tea Break	each	*24g*
Tyrol bar, Prewetts		*28g*

United	golden crunch/orange/mint	*21g*

Viennese fingers		*21g*
Viscount	mint/orange	*16g*

Wafer, not coated		*15g*
Wafer, pink filled		*7g*
Wafers for ice cream	see Ice creams and ice lollies	
Wagon wheels		*31g*
Water biscuits		*8g*
Wholemeal	bran	*15g*
	crispbread	*5g*
	shortbread	*15g*

YoYo	mint	*19g*
	toffee	*20g*

Biscuits, if name not specified = averages

Cheese biscuits		*4g*
Cream sandwich biscuits		*12g*
Full coated chocolate biscuits		*24g*
Semi-sweet biscuits	e.g. Marie	*7g*

Biscuits

11

Sweet biscuits	cookies, crunch	*10g*
Wafer biscuits	(cream filled, not ice-cream wafers)	*7g*

BREAD, ROLLS, CHAPATIS, ETC.

Bagel	plain	*70g*
Breadstick	each	*7g*
Brioche	individual	*45g*
Chapati	white or brown, average, without fat	*55g*
	with fat	*60g*
Croissant	chocolate, 'pain-au-chocolat'	*60g*
	mini	*35g*
	plain	*60g*
	savoury filled	*90g*
Croutons	with soup, homemade	*25g*
	purchased	*15g*
Crumpet	toasted	*40g*
Danish style light bread		
sliced	medium slice fresh	*20g*
	toasted	*18g*
French stick	2" slice	*40g*
	6" slice	*120g*
French toast	bread coated in egg, fried, 1 slice	*70g*
Garlic bread	1 slice	*20g*
	1 slice with cheese	*40g*
	restaurant portion	*60g*
Malt loaf	1 slice	*35g*
Muffin	white, toasted	*68g*
	wholemeal, toasted	*72g*
Naan bread	filled	*155g*
	plain	*160g*

Nimble, sliced	1 slice fresh	*20g*
	toasted	*18g*
Papadum	fried	*13g*
	grilled	*10g*
Paratha	plain	*140g*
	stuffed	*170g*
Pikelets	toasted, each	*25g*
Pitta bread	'mini', picnic	*35g*
	small	*75g*
	large	*95g*
Potato cake/bread	1 farl, fried	*65g*
	grilled	*56g*
Pumpernickel	1 average slice	*33g*
Puri, fried		*70g*
Rolls	bagel	*70g*
	bap, granary, white or wholemeal (6″ diameter)	*112g*
	bridge roll	*20g*
	granary roll	*56g*
	hamburger bun, bakers	*85g*
	prepacked	*50g*
	Hovis, 'mini loaf'	*40g*
	krisp roll e.g. Pogeus	*10g*
	white roll, crusty	*50g*
	soft	*45g*
	wholemeal roll, crusty	*48g*
	soft	*48g*
Roti, bread	cooked in tandoor	*100g*
Rye bread	1 average slice	*25g*
Slimcea, sliced	1 slice fresh	*15g*
	toasted	*13g*

Soda bread	1 farl	*130g*
Staffordshire oatcake		*50g*
Toasting loaf	white, 1 slice fresh	*27g*
	toasted	*24g*
White crusty bread	small loaf, 1 slice fresh	*27g*
	toasted	*24g*
	large loaf, 1 medium slice fresh	*35g*
	toasted	*31g*
	large loaf, 1 thick slice fresh	*50g*
	toasted	*45g*
White sliced bread	small loaf, 1 slice fresh	*25g*
(including Premium, soft-	toasted	*20g*
grain white loaves)	large loaf, 1 thin slice fresh	*31g*
	toasted	*22g*
	large loaf, 1 medium slice fresh	*36g*
	toasted	*27g*
	large loaf, 1 thick slice fresh	*44g*
	toasted	*34g*
Wholemeal sliced bread	small loaf, 1 slice fresh	*25g*
(including brown, granary,	toasted	*23g*
wheatgerm loaves)	large loaf, 1 medium slice fresh	*36g*
	toasted	*31g*
	large loaf, 1 thick slice fresh	*44g*
	toasted	*40g*
Wholemeal unsliced bread	small loaf, 1 average slice fresh	*30g*
	toasted	*27g*
	large loaf 1 medium slice fresh	*38g*
	toasted	*33g*
	large loaf, 1 thick slice fresh	*55g*
	toasted	*50g*

NB   For a thicker end crust of a loaf add on 10g.
Crusts are 30% of a slice in weight, e.g. a 30g slice weighs 21g without crust.
For fried bread, add on 10g fat per slice.

Breads

BREAKFAST CEREALS

All-Bran type cereals	e.g. Branbuds, Grapenuts, All-Bran	
	1 average portion, small	*30g*
	medium	*40g*
	large	*60g*
	1 tablespoon	*7g*
Clusters, Nestlé	1 average portion	*30g*
Cornflake type cereals	e.g. Branflakes, Weetaflakes, Frosties,	
	Crunchy Nut Cornflakes, Fruit and	
	Fibre, Golden Crackles	
	1 average portion, small	*20g*
	medium	*30g*
	large	*50g*
	1 tablespoon Branflakes	*8g*
	1 tablespoon Cornflakes	*6g*
	1 tablespoon Frosties	*8g*
	1 tablespoon Golden Crackles	*7g*
	1 variety pack, Cornflakes	*17g*
	Frosties/Crunchy Nut	
	Cornflakes	*23g*
	Golden Crackles	*25g*
Instant oat cereal	e.g. Ready Brek	
	made up weight,	
	average portion, small (⅙ pint milk)	*130g*
	medium (¼ pint milk)	*180g*
	large (⅓ pint milk)	*225g*
Lucky Charms, Nestlé		*30g*
Muesli cereals, not crunchy	e.g. Alpen, Country Store	
	1 average portion, small	*30g*
	medium	*50g*
	large	*80g*
	1 4oz cup muesli	*100g*
	1 sachet Alpen	*40g*
	1 tablespoon	*15g*

Muesli, crunchy	e.g. Original Crunchy, Harvest Crunch	
	1 average portion, small	*40g*
	medium	*60g*
	large	*100g*
	1 tablespoon	*20g*
Multi Cheerios, Nestlé	1 tablespoon	*5g*
Pop Tarts, Kelloggs	each	*52g*
Porridge	made up weight,	
	average portion, small	*110g*
	medium	*160g*
	large	*210g*
Puffed wheat	1 average portion	*20g*
	1 tablespoon	*3g*
Rice Krispie type cereals	e.g. Rice Krispies, Ricicles, Puffed Rice Cocopops, Special K	
	1 average portion, small	*20g*
	medium	*30g*
	large	*45g*
	1 tablespoon	*4g*
	1 variety pack, Cocopops	*30g*
	Rice Krispies	*20g*
	Ricicles	*30g*
Shredded Wheat, Nestlé	average portion (2)	*45g*
	each	*22g*
	Mini, average portion, small	*35g*
	medium	*45g*
	large	*70g*
Shreddies, Nestlé	average portion	*45g*
Splitz type cereal eg raisin	average portion, small	*25g*
	medium	*40g*
	large	*60g*
	1 tablespoon (7 pieces)	*9g*

Start multi-grain, Kelloggs	1 tablespoon (15 pieces)	*6g*
Sugar puff type cereals	e.g. Sugar Puffs, Smacks	
	1 average portion, small	*20g*
	medium	*30g*
	large	*50g*
	1 tablespoon	*6g*
Weetabix	1 bisk	*20g*

CAKES, BUNS AND PASTRIES

Almond slice		*35g*
American muffins	purchased	*85g*
Angel sandwich	purchased, average slice	*40g*
Apple and mincemeat tart	individual	*88g*
Apple strudel	slice	*115g*
Apple sundae		*53g*
Apple turnover	individual	*100g*
Bakewell tart	individual	*43g*
	slice of large tart	*120g*
Baklava, Greek pastry		*100g*
Banana cake	average slice	*85g*
Battenburg	purchased, average slice	*32g*
Belgian bun		*110g*
Black forest gateau	average portion	*90g*
Blackcurrant and apple slice		*32g*
Blackcurrant sundae		*55g*
Chelsea bun		*78g*
Cherry bakewell		*46g*
Cherry fruit cake	average slice	*42g*
Cherry slice		*38g*

Chocolate cake with buttercream	average slice	*65g*
	frozen, average slice	*35g*
Chocolate cupcake		*40g*
Chocolate eclair	bakery or home-made	*90g*
	purchased, frozen, fresh cream,	*35g*
Chocolate fancy, Lyons		*25g*
Chocolate fudge slice		*98g*
Chocolate krispie cake		*25g*
Chocolate mini roll		*25g*
Chocolate swirl, Lyons		*28g*
Choux bun	filled with cream	*112g*
Coconut cake	average slice	*40g*
Coconut crunch cake, Lyons		*27g*
Coconut pyramid		*25g*
Country slice		*38g*
Cream horn		*60g*
Cream slice		*100g*
Cupcakes, Lyons	purchased, iced	*39g*
Currant bun		*60g*
Custard tart	individual	*94g*
	slice of large tart	*140g*
Dairy cream sponge	average slice	*39g*

Danish pastry	large	*180g*
	medium	*110g*
Devonshire split		*65g*
Doughnut	apple filling	*85g*
	cream, custard filling	*75g*
	iced	*75g*
	jam filling	*75g*
	large, iced or filled	*130g*
	ring	*60g*
Eccles cake		*45g*
Fairy cake		*28g*
Flake cake		*31g*
Flapjack	medium slice	*60g*
	large slice	*90g*
Florentines		*60g*
French fancy	fondant fancy	*30g*
Fruit cake	plain, average slice, homemade	*90g*
	plain, average slice, purchased	*60g*
	rich, average slice	*70g*
	rich with marzipan and icing	*70g*
Fruit malt loaf		*35g*
Fruit pies	see Puddings and fruit pies	
Gateau with fresh cream	average slice	*85g*
	individual pot	*90g*
Gingerbread man		*50g*
Gingerbread, parkin		*50g*

Hot cross bun		*50g*
Iced bun		*65g*
Jam tart	individual	*34g*
	slice of large tart	*90g*
Jamaica ginger cake	average slice	*35g*
Lemon meringue pie	average slice	*150g*
	individual	*39g*
Macaroons		*28g*
Madeira	purchased, average slice	*40g*
Melting moment		*30g*
Meringue	with cream	*28g*
	without cream	*8g*
Mince pie	individual	*55g*
	slice of large pie	*90g*
Mini-roll	chocolate/vanilla	*25g*
	raspberry/vanilla	*27g*
Ostler, Lyons	any flavour	*30g*
Paklava, Greek pastry		*100g*
Rock cake		*45g*
Rum Baba		*198g*
Russian cake	sliced, average slice	*180g*
Scones	drop scones	*31g*
	plain, fruit, cheese	*48g*
	potato	*57g*
	wholemeal	*50g*
	with cream and jam, purchased	*50g*

Sponge cake	no fat, with cream, purchased	*58g*
	with fat, with buttercream filling,	
	average slice	*60g*
	with fat, with jam filling,	
	average slice	*60g*
Sponge finger	each	*4g*
Sultana cake	purchased, average slice	*50g*
Swiss bun		*50g*
Swiss roll	average slice	*30g*
Teacake	fresh	*60g*
	toasted	*55g*
Treacle tart	individual	*35g*
Trifle sponge		*24g*
Vanilla slice		*113g*
Viennese slice	average	*34g*
Viennese split	each	*16g*
Viennese whirl	each	*27g*
Welsh cakes		*28g*

Cakes

CHEESE AND CHEESE DISHES

Cheese

Camembert type cheese	⅙ portion	*40g*
	average portion	*40g*
Cauliflower cheese	average portion, main dish	*200g*
	side dish	*90g*
	frozen purchased ready meal, for one	*235g*
Cheddar type cheese	chunk, small	*20g*
	medium	*40g*
	large	*60g*
	grated, 1 tablespoon	*10g*
	matchbox size piece	*30g*
	pick 'n' mix, each	*20g*
	in ploughmans lunch, average	*120g*
	in sandwich, average (cheese only)	*45g*
Cheese and egg flan	1 slice	*120g*
Cheese and onion pastie		*125g*
Cheese triangle	small, Dairylea	*14g*
	Laughing Cow	*17g*
	large, Dairylea chunky	*25g*
Cottage cheese	1 small pot	*112g*
	1 tablespoon	*40g*
	in sandwich	*50g*
Cream cheese	pick 'n' mix, each	*17g*
	in sandwich, average	*30g*
Crispy cheese pancake	purchased frozen, fried	*68g*
Danish blue	average portion	*30g*
Edam/Gouda type	average portion	*40g*
Fromage frais	see Yoghurt and fromage frais	

Low fat soft cheese, Quark	1 heaped tablespoon	*55g*
Macaroni cheese	average portion	*220g*
	canned, large tin	*430g*
	small tin	*210g*
Mini baby bel	each	*18g*
Pizza	chilled/frozen, large	*350–500g*
	medium	*200g*
	frozen, fun size	*40g*
	individual slices	*100g*
	small	*100g*
	homemade, average portion	*300g*

Pizza, deep pan

5″ diameter	average, cheese & tomato	*116g*
	meat/fish	*160g*
	vegetarian	*150g*
	'special'	*190g*
6″ diameter, children's	average, cheese & tomato	*220g*
7″ diameter (serves 1)	average, cheese & tomato	*230g*
	meat/fish	*290g*
	vegetarian	*300g*
	'special'	*360g*
	1 slice = ¼ of total weight of pizza	
9–10″ diameter (serves 1–2)	average, cheese & tomato	*410g*
	meat/fish	*500g*
	vegetarian	*500g*
	'special'	*580g*
	1 slice = ⅙ of total weight of pizza	
12″ diameter (serves 2–3)	average, cheese & tomato	*700g*
	meat/fish	*800g*
	vegetarian	*800g*
	'special'	*890g*
	1 slice = ⅛ of total weight of pizza	

Cheese

Pizza, thin crust

7″ diameter (serves 1)	average, cheese & tomato	*116g*
	meat/fish	*150g*
	vegetarian	*150g*
	'special'	*190g*
	1 slice = ¼ of total weight of pizza	
9–10″ diameter (serves 1–2)	average, cheese & tomato	*260g*
	meat/fish	*310g*
	vegetarian	*340g*
	'special'	*350g*
	1 slice = ⅙ of total weight of pizza	
12″ diameter (serves 2–3)	average, cheese & tomato	*560g*
	meat/fish	*660g*
	'special'	*740g*
	vegetarian	*660g*
	1 slice = ⅛ of total weight of pizza	

Average weights of extra toppings, per individual medium pizza (10″ thin crust, 7″ deep pan)

	anchovies	*10g*
	cheese	*30g*
	ham, bacon, pepperoni, salami, sausage	*30g*
	mushroom, pepper, onion, sweetcorn	*30g*
	pineapple	*60g*
	spicy beef, chicken	*30g*
	tuna, olives	*15g*

Processed cheese	1 slice	*20g*
	1 triangle, small	*14g*
	Dairylea, Laughing Cow	*17g*
	1 triangle, large, Dairylea chunky	*25g*

Stilton		*35g*

Vol au vents	filled with cheese sauce, 1 small	*30g*

Welsh rarebit	topping only	*40g*
	with toast, 1 slice	*67g*

CONFECTIONERY

Aero milk chocolate, Nestlé		
Rowntree	bar	*48g*
	chunky bar	*37g*
	snack size	*28g*
	mini	*11g*
After Eight mints, Nestlé		
Rowntree	each	*8g*
American hard gums	tube	*45g*
	each	*4g*
Aniseed balls	each	*4g*
Applause, Mars	standard bar	*50g*
	fun size	*24g*
Barker and Dobson menthol		
BPC	each	*8g*
Barley sugar	piece	*7g*
Barratt's everlasting toffee		
strip		*22g*
Barratt's French nougat	bar	*114g*
Barratt's fruit drops	box	*115g*
	small packet	*56g*
	each	*16g*
Bassett's jelly babies	box	*115g*
	small packet	*56g*
Bassett's liquorice Allsorts	box	*115g*
	small packet	*56g*
	each	*5g*
Bettabar	bar	*30g*
Black Magic, Nestlé		
Rowntree	chocolate assortment, each	*8g*
Blackjacks	each	*4g*
Bon bons	packet	*113g*
Boost bars, Cadbury's	Biscuit Boost	*57g*
	snack size	*36g*
	treat size	*21g*
	Coconut Boost	*53g*
Bounty bar, Mars	plain/milk, twin	*57g*
	mini	*29g*

Bournville chocolate, Cadbury's	small bar	*50g*
Bournville Fruit & Nut bar, Cadbury's		*100g*
Brazil nut chocolates	each	*12g*
Bubble gum	average each	*4g*
	bubble hamburger	*6g*
	Bubblicious	*5g*
	High blow	*8g*
	Hubba bubba	*6g*
	Super bazooka	*8g*
Buttermints	each	*7g*
Butterscotch	packet	*133g*
Buttons, chocolate, Cadbury's	large packet	*51g*
	standard packet	*33g*
	4 buttons	*5g*
	treat size	*14g*
	creamy white buttons, packet	*32g*

Cadbury's Bar Six		*40g*
Cadbury's Caramel	bar	*50g*
	treat size	*17g*
Cadbury's Caramel Egg		*40g*
Cadbury's Chomp		*26g*
Cadbury's Creme Egg		*39g*
	mini	*12g*
Cadbury's Crunchie		*42g*
	treat size	*17g*
Cadbury's Curly Wurly		*29g*
Cadbury's Dairy Milk chocolate	standard bar	*54g*
	snack size	*30g*
	vending	*43g*
	miniatures	*5g*
	square	*7g*
	treat size	*15g*
Cadbury's Double Decker	standard bar	*51g*
	treat size	*19g*
Cadbury's Flake	bar	*34g*
	99, treat size, finger	*9g*

Cadbury's Finger of Fudge	bar	*30g*
	treat size	*15g*
Cadbury's Fruit & Nut milk		
chocolate	standard	*52g*
	snack	*30g*
Cadbury's Golden Crisp		*100g*
Cadbury's Mini Eggs	packet	*85g*
	each	*3g*
Cadbury's Nut Crisp	bar	*44g*
Cadbury's Old Jamaica		*100g*
Cadbury's Picnic	bar	*49g*
	snack	*29g*
Cadbury's Shoe People		*15g*
Cadbury's Snack	6 shortbread	*42g*
	1 shortbread	*7g*
Cadbury's Spira	finger	*20g*
Cadbury's Tasters	packet	*45g*
Cadbury's Tiffin		*100g*
Cadbury's Time Out bar	bar	*40g*
	finger	*20g*
	treat size	*20g*
Cadbury's Top Deck		*100g*
Cadbury's Twirl	bar	*44g*
	finger	*22g*
	treat size	*22g*
Cadbury's Strollers	packet	*45g*
Cadbury's Whole Nut	standard	*51g*
	snack size	*30g*
Cadbury's Wildlife	bar	*22g*
Cadbury's Wispa	standard	*39g*
	snack size	*23g*
	treat size	*15g*
Caramac, Nestlé		
Rowntree	bar	*30g*
	per square	*3g*
Chewetts	packet	*18g*
	each	*3g*
Chewing gum	average packet	*18g*
	stick	*2g*
Chews, fruit salad	each	*4g*
Chewy mints	tube	*39g*
	each	*3g*

Chocolate almonds	each	*3g*
Chocolate assortments, Cadbury's	each	*10g*
Chocolate brazils	each	*12g*
Chocolate covered ginger	each	*8g*
Chocolate eclairs	tube	*46g*
	each	*9g*
Chocolate mice	large, each	*6g*
	small, each	*3g*
Chocolate nuts, M & M's, Mars	packet	*47g*
Chocolate orange/mint crisp	each	*10g*
Chocolate orange, Terry's	bar	*49g*
Clear mints	glacier mints, tube	*38g*
Coconut Grove		*55g*
Coconut ice		*125g*
Cola bottles	(jelly), each	*3g*
Cola sweets	each	*4g*
Cote D'or chocolate	1 square	*8g*
Creamy fudge	1 inch square	*11g*
Crunch, Nestlé Rowntree	bar	*31g*
Crunch, Milk, Nestlé Rowntree	bar	*33g*

Dextrosol	glucose tablet, each	*7g*
Dime bar		*30g*
	snack size	*13g*
Dolly mixtures	box	*115g*
	bag	*56g*
Drifter bar, Nestlé Rowntree	standard size	*56g*
	per finger	*28g*

Edinburgh rock	average stick	*100g*
Eggs	Cadbury's caramel egg, each	*40g*
	Cadbury's mini creme egg, each	*12g*
	Cadbury's mini eggs, each	*3g*
	Creme eggs, each	*39g*
	Nutcracker, Terry's per half shell	*18g*
	Truffle eggs, Galaxy per half shell	*17g*
Everton mints	each	*6g*
Extra strong mints, Trebor	tube	*51g*

Fisherman's Friend throat lozenges	each	*1g*
Fizzers	packet	*4g*
Flump	pink marshmallow shape, each	*2g*
Fruit bon bons	each	*7g*
Fruit drops	tube	*16g*
Fruit gums, Nestlé Rowntree	tube	*40g*
	each	*2g*
Fruit pastilles, Nestlé Rowntree	tube	*42g*
	mini	*18g*
	each	*3g*
Fruit salad chews	each	*4g*
Fruitellas	tube	*34g*
	each	*4g*
Fry's chocolate cream	bar	*50g*
Fry's turkish delight	bar	*51g*
Fudge	no additions, 1 inch square	*11g*
Fudge finger, Cadbury's		*30g*
	treat size	*15g*

Galaxy	bar	*47g*
Galaxy Gold	bar	*43g*
Galaxy truffle egg		*34g*
Ginger, chocolate covered	each	*8g*
Glacier fruits	tube	*38g*
Glacier mints	clear mints, tube	*38g*
	each	*3g*
Gobstoppers	each	*8g*
Golden cup bar, Nestlé Rowntree	large	*60g*
	standard	*37g*
	small	*22g*

Hacks, throat lozenges	each	*3g*
Hall mentholyptus	packet	*32g*
Halo Chocolate, reduced calorie	bar	*29g*
Haribo Gummi bears	packet	*125g*
Hazel whirls	each	*8g*
Highland toffee bar		*15g*
Humbugs	each	*8g*

Jelly animal	each	*12g*
Jelly babies, Bassetts	box	*113g*
	small bag	*56g*
	each	*6g*
Jelly beans	each	*3g*
Jelly bears, Gummi bears	packet	*125g*
Jelly bottles	each	*3g*
Jelly shapes	each	*5g*
Jelly tots, Nestlé Rowntree	packet	*43g*
	mini pack	*25g*
	each	*1g*
Kit Kat, Nestlé Rowntree	4 fingers	*49g*
	2 fingers	*22g*
KP chocolate/toffee dips		*34g*
	biscuits	*17g*
	dip	*17g*
Krunch	bar	*31g*
Lion bar, Nestlé Rowntree	standard size	*53g*
	snack size	*34g*
	mini	*16g*
Liqueur chocolates	each	*8g*
Liquorice Allsorts, Bassetts	box	*113g*
	small bag	*56g*
Liquorice shoelace	each	*6g*
Liquorice sticks	each	*3g*
Liquorice toffees	each	*8g*
Liquorice torpedoes	packet	*76g*
	6 torpedoes	*10g*
Lockets throat lozenges	packet	*43g*
Logger fruit and nut chocolate, Terry's	bar	*50g*
Logger milk chocolate, Terry's	bar	*50g*
Lollipops	each	*5g*
Lovehearts	packet	*16g*
Lucozade tablets	each	*4g*
M & M's, Mars	plain	*45g*
	peanut	*47g*
	plain/peanut, family bag	*120g*

Mac throat lozenges	each	*3g*
Maltesers, Mars	family bag	*80g*
	standard bag	*37g*
	each	*2g*
	funsize	*21g*
Mars almond snack bar		*38g*
Mars bar	kingsize	*100g*
	standard	*65g*
	snack	*42g*
	funsize	*19g*
Marshmallows	each	*5g*
	bag	*40g*
Marzipan fruits	each	*12g*
Matchmakers	each	*2g*
Milk chew	each	*4g*
Milk chocolate assortment	each	*10g*
Milk chocolate bar	average	*50g*
	1 square	*7g*
Milk chocolate raisins	packet	*44g*
	each	*2g*
Milk gums	each	*2g*
Milkybar	chunky	*37g*
	large	*33g*
	medium	*20g*
	standard	*13g*
Milkybar buttons, Nestlé Rowntree	bag	*30g*
Milky Way, Mars	standard	*26g*
	funsize	*17g*
Minstrels, Galaxy	family bag	*100g*
	bag	*42g*
	each	*3g*
Mint imperials	each	*2g*
Minties, Nestlé Rowntree	tube	*44g*
	each	*4g*
Mintolas, Nestlé Rowntree	standard tube	*62g*
	mini tube	*21g*
	each	*4g*
Mints, Trebor	extra strong, per tube	*51g*
	extra strong, each	*3g*
Moments, Terry's	bar	*48g*

Murray fruits, Murray mints	tube	*50g*
	each	*5g*
Munchies, Nestlé Rowntree	standard tube	*55g*
	mini tube	*18g*
	each	*5g*
Munchies, Nestlé Rowntree, hazlenut	tube	*57g*
	each	*5g*
Neapolitans	Terry's nap, each	*8g*
Newberry fruits	each	*9g*
Noisette cup	each	*8g*
Nougat	large bar	*114g*
	small bar	*70g*
	sweet	*10g*
Opal fruits	packet	*114g*
	tube	*45g*
	fun size	*21g*
	each	*4g*
Orange and lemon slices	each	*5g*
Orbit gum	stick	*2g*
Parma violets	packet	*16g*
	each	*1g*
Pastilles, fruit, Nestlé Rowntree	tube	*40g*
	each	*3g*
Peanut brittle	bar	*58g*
Pear drops	large, each	*6g*
	small, each	*2g*
Penny chew	each	*4g*
Peppermint creams	not chocolate covered	*6g*
	chocolate covered	*7g*
Pineapple chunks	each	*5g*
Polo fruits, Nestlé Rowntree	tube	*30g*
Polo mints, Nestlé Rowntree	tube	*30g*
	mini tube	*13g*
	each	*2g*
Pontefract cakes	each	*4g*
Poppets, Paynes	box	*45g*
Pyramint, Terry's		*30g*

Quality Street, Nestlé		
Rowntree	chocolate assortment, each	*8g*
Refreshers	tube	*14g*
	each	*1g*
Revels, Mars	family packet	*105g*
	packet	*35g*
	each	*2g*
Ripple bar, Galaxy		*22g*
Ritter chocolate bars	all types	*100g*
Rock	1 average stick	*100g*
Rolo Egg, Nestlé Rowntree	each	*34g*
Rolos, Nestlé Rowntree	tube	*58g*
	mini tube	*27g*
	each	*5g*
Ruffle bar, Cadbury's		*28g*
Rum and raisin fudge	1 square inch	*11g*
Rum and raisin toffee	each	*8g*
Secret, Nestlé Rowntree	bar	*39g*
Sesame snaps	packet	*30g*
Sherbet bon bons	each	*7g*
Sherbet Dib Dab, Barratts	lolly	*5g*
	sherbet	*14g*
Sherbet Fountain, Swizzles	sherbet	*24g*
	liquorice	*5g*
Sherbet lolly		*5g*
Sherbet pips	each	*1g*
Skittles	family bag	*125g*
	packet	*60g*
	fun size	*23g*
Smarties, Nestlé Rowntree	tube	*37g*
	mini box	*15g*
Snickers bar, Mars	king size	*100g*
	standard	*61g*
	snack bar	*38g*
	fun size	*19g*
Soft mints	tube	*45g*
Strepsils throat lozenges	each	*3g*
Suchard chocolate bars	standard	*100g*
Suchard praline milk		
chocolate bar		*42g*

Confectionery

Suchard Toblerone	very large	*400g*
	large	*200g*
	medium	*100g*
	small	*50g*
	mini	*35g*
Sugared almonds	each	*6g*
Sweet cigarette	each	*7g*

Tasters, Cadbury's	bag	*45g*
Terry's Bitz	bar	*50g*
Terry's Chocolate orange, milk/plain	bar	*49g*
Terry's Crispy Caramel		*45g*
Terry's Logger	bar	*50g*
Terry's Moments	bar	*48g*
Terry's Neapolitans, 'naps'	each	*8g*
Terry's Orange chocolate	1 piece	*9g*
Terry's plain chocolate bar	large	*150g*
	medium	*100g*
	small	*50g*
Terry's plain chocolate bar with marzipan		*41g*
Terry's Waifa bar	plain or milk chocolate	*35g*
Throat pastilles	each	*2g*
Tic-Tacs	box	*12g*
Toblerone, Suchard	large	*200g*
	medium	*100g*
	small	*50g*
	mini	*35g*
Toffee Cup		*23g*
Toffee Crisp, Nestlé Rowntree	standard	*48g*
	snack size	*33g*
	mini	*18g*
Toffee egg		*20g*
Toffees	not chocolate covered, no additions, each	*8g*
Toffos, plain/mint/assorted	tube	*47g*
	each	*5g*
Tooty Frooties	bag	*41g*
Topic	bar	*47g*

Tracker	standard bar	*37g*
	grocer pack (6 pack), each	*27g*
Tracker buttermunch		*18g*
Trebor mints	packet	*28g*
Trebor soft fruits	packet	*45g*
Tunes throat lozenges	packet	*37g*
	each	*3g*
Turkish delight, Fry's	chocolate covered bar	*51g*
Turkish delight	1 square	*15g*
Twix, Mars	standard	*56g*
	single finger	*28g*
	mini	*21g*
Twix, Tea breaks		*28g*

Victory V's	packet	*50g*
Vice Versa, Nestlé Rowntree	packet	*47g*

Walnut Whip, Nestlé Rowntree	each	*32g*
Wine gums	each	*3g*
Wrigley's chewing gum	stick	*2g*

XXX Mints	tube	*48g*
	each	*3g*

Yes	packet	*37g*
Yoghurt coated peanuts and raisins	each	*1g*
Yorkie, almond, Nestlé Rowntree		*60g*
Yorkie milk chocolate bar, Nestlé Rowntree		*66g*
	1 chunk	*10g*
Yorkie, raisin and biscuit, Nestlé Rowntree		*61g*

EGG AND EGG DISHES

Egg custard	average portion	*140g*
Egg, duck's	boiled, no shell, average size	*75g*
Egg fried rice	average portion	*270g*
Egg, hen's	boiled, no shell, average size	*50g*
	no shell, size 1	*67g*
	no shell, size 2	*61g*
	no shell, size 3	*57g*
	no shell, size 4	*47g*
	dried egg, 1 tablespoon	*5g*
Egg, hen's, white	average size	*32g*
Egg, hen's, yolk	average size	*18g*
Egg mayonnaise	average portion	*120g*
Fried egg	average	*60g*
Omelette	2 eggs	*120g*
Poached egg	average size	*50g*
Quiche	average slice, small, (¼ purchased quiche)	*95g*
	medium	*140g*
	large	*180g*
	mini	*40g*
Scotch egg	average size	*120g*
	mini, picnic egg	*60g*
Scrambled egg	2 eggs	*120g*
Soufflé	average portion	*110g*
Yorkshire pudding	see Pasta, rice and grains	

FATS

Butter or hard margarine	average spread on slice of bread, thin	*7g*
	medium	*10g*
	thick	*12g*
	average spread on roll, thin	*10g*
	medium	*12g*
	thick	*15g*
	average spread on toasted crumpet	*15g*
	1 curl	*8g*
	1 portion, packed	*10g*
	1 restaurant portion, not packed	*20g*
	1 teaspoon	*5g*
Butter in 'boil in the bag'		*15g*
Butter/margarine in baked potato		*20g*
Flora	1 portion pack	*10g*
Oil	1 tablespoon	*11g*
	1 teaspoon	*3g*
Margarine, soft; low fat spread	average spread on slice of bread, thin	*5g*
	medium	*7g*
	thick	*10g*
	average spread on roll, thin	*7g*
	medium	*10g*
	thick	*12g*
	average spread on toasted crumpet	*10g*
	thin scraping on crispbread	*2g*
	1 teaspoon	*5g*

NB For toast add 2g spread per slice

FISH AND FISH PRODUCTS

Unless specified, weights are edible portion.

Anchovy	1 anchovy	*3g*
	1 small tin	*50g*
	average on pizza	*10g*
Caviar	1 tablespoon	*19g*
Cockle	1 cockle	*4g*
	small jar	*142g*
	average portion	*25g*
Cod	1 average fillet, small	*50g*
	medium	*120g*
	large	*175g*
	1 average steak	*50g*
	in batter, small	*120g*
	medium	*180g*
	large	*225g*
	in batter or crumb, oven crispy	*100g*
	in sauce, purchased, frozen	*170g*
Cod roe	average portion fried or grilled	*116g*
	in batter, average portion	*160g*
Conger eel	average portion, grilled with bones	*225g*
	without bones	*115g*
Crab	1 tablespoon crab meat	*40g*
	1 small can	*85g*
	1 large can	*170g*
	1 average dressed crab, no shell	*130g*
Crabstick	1 stick	*17g*
Dogfish	see rock salmon	
Dover sole	1 whole, average, with bone	*250g*

Eel	1 slice, 5″ long	*20g*
	average portion	*70g*
Filet-o-fish	McDonald's	*156g*
Fish and pasta bake	purchased ready meal, average	*275g*
Fish cakes	1 fried in batter	*100g*
	1 frozen, fried or grilled	*50g*
Fish fingers	1 fish finger, fried or grilled	*28g*
	1 jumbo size fish finger	*60g*
Fish in a bun	BurgerKing, Ocean Catch (bun and fish)	*175g*
	fried fish in a bun, fish only	*75g*
Fish in batter	fast food outlet, average	*160g*
	fish and chip shop, average	*170g*
Fish in sauce	frozen, purchased	*170g*
Fish lasagne	purchased ready meal for one, average	*290g*
Fish paste	1 small jar	*35g*
	1 medium jar	*53g*
	1 large jar	*75g*
	average spread on slice of bread	*10g*
Fish paté	average portion, as starter	*40g*
Fish pie	(fish and pastry)	
	average serving	*170g*
	(fish and potato, not pastry)	
	average serving	*250g*
	purchased frozen ready meal for one	*320g*
Grey mullet	1 average whole, grilled	*100g*
Haddock	1 grilled fillet, small	*50g*
	medium	*120g*
	large	*170g*

	1 average fillet fried in batter, small	*120g*
	medium	*170g*
	large	*220g*
	1 average fillet, oven baked	*100g*
	1 average fillet, purchased	
	breadcrumbed, fried or grilled	*120g*
	1 average fillet, smoked, poached	*150g*
Hake	1 average steak	*100g*
Halibut	average portion, poached	*110g*
	1 average steak, grilled	*145g*
Herring	1 filleted, small	*85g*
	medium	*119g*
	filleted in tomato sauce, 1 can	*200g*
	pickled, 1 roll mop herring	*90g*
Herring roe	average portion fried or grilled	*85g*
Hoki	1 average fillet, grilled	*190g*
Kedgeree	average portion	*300g*
King prawn	1, no shell	*8g*
Kipper	1 grilled fillet, small	*85g*
	medium	*130g*
	large	*170g*
	1 'Boil-in-the-bag', with butter	*170g*
	1 can kipper fillets	*200g*
Lemon sole	1 average, grilled or fried or steamed,	
	small	*100g*
	medium	*170g*
	large	*220g*
Lobster	average portion, 2 tablespoons	*85g*
	half dressed lobster, with shell	*250g*
Mackerel	1 whole fried mackerel	*220g*
	average portion grilled mackerel	*160g*

	1 average smoked mackerel, small	*100g*
	medium	*150g*
	large	*200g*
	1 can mackerel in oil,	
	small can	*200g*
	large can	*425g*
	1 can mackerel in curry/tomato/mustard	
	sauce	*125g*

Monkfish	average portion, grilled	*70g*

Mussels	1 mussel, no shell	*7g*
	1 average portion, no shells	*40g*
	1 jar mussels small	*80g*
	large	*198g*
	1 small tin smoked mussels	*105g*

Oysters	1 oyster with shell	*42g*
	1 oyster without shell	*10g*
	1 dozen oysters, edible portion	*120g*
	1 can smoked oysters	*105g*

Paella	frozen, purchased	*284g*

Pilchards	1 canned pilchard in tomato sauce	*55g*
	1 can pilchards, small	*215g*
	large	*425g*

Plaice	1 average fillet plaice, steamed or grilled,	
	small	*75g*
	medium	*130g*
	large	*180g*
	1 average fillet plaice, in breadcrumbs,	
	fried, small	*90g*
	medium	*150g*
	large	*200g*
	1 average fillet plaice, in batter, fried,	
	small	*150g*
	medium	*200g*
	large	*250g*

	1 average whole plaice in batter or crumb, oven ready	112g
	1 average whole stuffed plaice, purchased frozen	190g
Prawns	1 prawn, without shell	3g
	1 average portion prawns, shelled	60g
	1 king prawn, without shell	8g
	half a pint of prawns, shelled	142g
	prawn cocktail	88g
	prawns	40g
	lettuce	20g
	cocktail sauce	28g
	1 small jar prawns	100g
Rainbow trout	1 average, grilled,	
	with bones and head	230g
	without bones and head	155g
Red mullet	1 average whole, grilled	75g
Red snapper	1 average whole, fried	200g
Rock salmon (dogfish)	1 average portion in batter, fried,	
	small	150g
	medium	200g
	large	250g
Roe	1 average portion cod's roe, grilled or fried	116g
	1 average portion cod's roe in batter	160g
	1 average portion herring roe, fried or grilled	85g
Salmon	1 average salmon steak, steamed or poached	100g
	1 large salmon steak, grilled	170g
	1 average portion canned salmon	100g
	1 average portion canned salmon in a sandwich	45g
	1 average portion smoked salmon	56g

Sardines	6 average, grilled	*86g*
	1 average portion canned sardines	*100g*
	1 average portion in sandwich	*50g*
	1 canned sardine	*25g*
Scampi	1 average portion of scampi, fried in breadcrumbs	*170g*
	1 piece scampi, crumb coated	*15g*
Seafood tagliatelle	purchased ready meal for one	*235g*
Shrimps	potted, average portion	*50g*
Skate	1 average large wing, grilled	*290g*
	1 average portion skate, fried in batter	*200g*
	1 average portion skate, cooked in butter	*150g*
Sprats	1 portion sprats, fried or grilled with bones	*220g*
	1 sprat fried or grilled with bones	*55g*
Squid	1 average portion cooked squid	*65g*
	1 average ring of squid, fried in batter (calamari)	*20g*
	1 average portion fried squid in batter	*120g*
Swordfish	1 average portion, grilled	*140g*
Taramasalata	average portion, 1 tablespoon	*45g*
	1 average tub, purchased	*112g*
Trout	1 average trout, fried or grilled, with bones and head	*230g*
	without bones and head	*155g*
	1 average stuffed trout	*270g*
Tuna	1 average portion for sandwich filling	*45g*
	1 average portion with salad	*92g*
	1 small can	*100g*
Turbot	1 average whole, grilled	*160g*

Fish

45

Whelks	1 whelk, without shell	*7g*
	1 average portion whelks	*30g*
White fish	(If type not specified)	
	small fillet	*100g*
	medium fillet	*150g*
	large fillet	*180g*
Whitebait	1 whitebait, fried in flour	*4g*
	1 average portion, fried	*80g*
Whiting	1 average portion, fried in batter,	
	small	*120g*
	medium	*180g*
	large	*240g*
	1 average portion, steamed	*85g*

FRUIT

Apple	1 raw small eating (6 to lb) with core	75g
	without core	67g
	1 raw medium eating (4 to lb)	112g
	without core	100g
	1 raw large eating (2–3 to lb)	170g
	without core	153g
	stewed with sugar, average portion	110g
	without sugar, average portion	85g
	1 baked, average portion	190g
Apricot	1 raw without stone	40g
	canned with syrup/juice, average portion	140g
	1 dried	8g
Avocado pear	1 raw small without skin or stone	100g
	1 raw medium without skin or stone	145g
	1 raw large without skin or stone	195g
	average ½ pear	75g
Banana	1 raw small without skin	80g
	1 raw medium without skin	100g
	1 raw large without skin	120g
	1 raw slice without skin	5g
	10 dried chips	13g
Bilberries	1 raw	2g
Blackberries	1 raw	5g
	stewed with sugar, average portion	140g
Blackcurrants	5 raw	2g
	Stewed with sugar, average portion	140g
Cherries	1 raw eating without stone	4g
Clementines	1 raw small without skin	40g
	1 raw medium without skin	60g
	1 raw large without skin	80g

Fruit

Currants	4 dried	*1g*
	1 heaped tablespoon, dried	*25g*
Damson	1 raw without stone	*15g*
Date	1 raw without stone	*25g*
	1 dried without stone	*15g*
Fig	1 raw	*55g*
	1 dried	*20g*
Fruit juices	see Beverages	
Fruit salad	canned with syrup or juice average portion	*115g*
	fresh with syrup or juice, average portion	*140g*
Gooseberries	stewed with sugar, average portion	*140g*
Grapes	1 raw	*5g*
	1 seedless	*2g*
	small bunch	*100g*
Grapefruit	1 raw small with skin	*250g*
	1 raw medium with skin	*340g*
	1 raw large with skin	*425g*
	½, raw flesh only	*80g*
	canned with syrup or juice, average portion	*120g*
Greengage	1 raw without stone	*50g*
Kiwi fruit	1 raw medium without skin	*60g*
Kumquat	1 raw medium	*8g*
Lemon	juice from ½ lemon	*10g*
	1 slice for drinks	*20g*
Loquat	1 raw without stone	*13g*

Lychee	1 raw without stone or skin	*15g*
	canned without stone	*13g*
Mandarin orange	no skin, small	*60g*
	medium	*100g*
	large	*140g*
Mango	1 without stone or peel	*150g*
	1 slice	*40g*
	canned in syrup average portion	*105g*
Medlar	1 raw, without stone	*60g*
Melon	canteloupe, 1 slice without skin	*150g*
	honeydew, 1 slice without skin	*200g*
	watermelon, 1 slice without skin	*200g*
Mineola	average with skin	*200g*
Mixed dried fruit	1 heaped tablespoon	*25g*
Nectarine	1 raw average without stone	*90g*
Olive	without stone, stuffed olive	*3g*
Orange	1 raw small without skin	*120g*
	1 raw medium without skin	*160g*
	1 raw large without skin	*210g*
	juice from 1 orange	*55g*
Passion fruit	1 average, flesh and seeds only	*15g*
Paw paw (papaya)	1 average slice, without skin or stone	*140g*
Peach	1 raw small without stone	*70g*
	1 raw medium without stone	*110g*
	1 raw large without stone	*150g*
	canned with syrup or juice, average portion	*120g*

Fruit

Pear	comice, 1 raw medium	*150g*
	large	*250g*
	conference, 1 raw medium	*170g*
	canned, ½ pear	*60g*
	canned with syrup or juice, average portion	*135g*
Pineapple	1 raw large slice without skin	*80g*
	canned, one ring, or 6 chunks	*40g*
	1 fritter	*60g*
Plum	raw, small without stone	*30g*
	medium without stone	*55g*
	large without stone	*85g*
Prunes	1 dried, with stone	*8g*
	6 stewed, without stones	*60g*
Raisins	1 tablespoon dried	*30g*
Raspberries	1 raw	*4g*
	raw, average portion (15 raspberries)	*60g*
	canned with syrup or juice, average portion	*90g*
Rhubarb	stewed, with sugar, average portion	*140g*
Satsuma	see tangerine	
Sharon fruit	1 raw	*110g*
Strawberry	1 raw	*12g*
	raw, average portion	*100g*
	canned with syrup, average portion	*90g*
Sultanas	1 tablespoon, dried	*30g*
Tangerine	1 raw small without skin	*50g*
	1 raw medium without skin	*70g*
	1 raw large without skin	*90g*

ICE-CREAMS AND ICE-LOLLIES

Bombe	chocolate covered, individual	*60g*
Bomboniera, Walls		*73g*
Bounty, Mars	twin	*48g*
	single	*24g*
Calippo, Walls		*139g*
Catering Brickette	strawberry; vanilla (Walls)	*36g*
Choc ice	Cadbury's Dairy Milk (Nestlé)	*56g*
	Chunky (Walls)	*50g*
	Classico (Nestlé)	*44g*
	Dark and golden (Walls)	*48g*
	Kick (Walls)	*58g*
Cones/cornets (no ice cream)	large	*4g*
	medium	*3g*
	square	*4g*
	sugar	*11g*
Cornetto, Walls	choc 'n' nut	*73g*
	dairy cappuccino	*73g*
	mint choc chip	*75g*
	strawberry	*81g*
Diddy Tub, Walls	strawberry; vanilla	*41g*
Elite Tub, Walls	chocolate; strawberry; vanilla	*140g*
Fab, Nestlé		*61g*
Feast, Walls	chocolate, mint	*85g*
	nutty	*97g*
Frozen yoghurt	average portion	*56g*
Galaxy Dove, Mars		*104g*
Hooded skull, Walls		*65g*
Ice-cream	average serving	*75g*
	1 average scoop	*60g*
	block, 1 average slice	*75g*
	tub	*60g*
	individual slices, vanilla	*36g*
	bar, Golden vanilla (Walls)	*48g*

King Cone, Nestlé	vanilla and strawberry	*81g*
	vanilla, chocolate and nuts	*89g*
	mint choc chip	*75g*
Kulfi	Indian ice-cream, average	*80g*
Magnifico, Walls		*117g*
Magnum, Walls	almond	*96g*
	dark; white chocolate	*94g*
Mars bar, Mars		*57g*
Max, Walls	banana; caramel	*59g*
	chocolate; toffee; vanilla	*70g*
Milky Way, Mars		*19g*
Mincemeat Brulee, Walls		*108g*
Mini Juice, Walls	apple; orange	*36g*
Mini Milk, Walls	chocolate; strawberry; vanilla	*30g*
Mini Yogice, Walls	banana; strawberry	*33g*
Mint crisp, Nestlé		*70g*
Mivvi, Nestlé	pineapple and cream	*63g*
	raspberry and cream	*65g*
Mr Men, Nestlé	all types except dairy	*45g*
	dairy	*40g*
Opals Iced fruits, Mars		*99g*
Orange Fruitie, Walls		*82g*
Orange Maid		*71g*
Penguin ice-cream bar, Mars		*56g*
Romantica, Walls	1 average slice	*60g*
Screwball, Treats		*67g*
Scribbler, Walls		*45g*
Sky, Walls		*52g*
Snickers, Mars		*57g*
Sparkles, Walls	lemonade; orange	*57g*
Strawberry Split, Walls		*77g*
Tangle Twister, Walls		*80g*
Toffee Crumble, Nestlé		*56g*
Too Good To Be True, Walls	average scoop	*62g*
Tub, ice-cream		*61g*
Twix, Mars		*57g*

Vanilla	bar	*49g*
Viennetta, Walls	1 average slice	*56g*
	individual	*55g*
Wafers	each	*2g*
	cups	*4g*
	fan	*5g*
Whippy ice-cream, Walls	in medium cone	*53g*
Zoom, Nestlé		*63g*

Meat

Bacon	1 rasher back bacon, fried or grilled	
	average	*25g*
	1 rasher middle bacon, fried or grilled	
	average	*40g*
	1 rasher streaky bacon, fried or grilled	
	average	*20g*
	1 portion bacon average	*46g*
	1 gammon steak average	*170g*
	in a bun, average	*100g*
	with egg in a bun, average	*120g*
	Burger King,	
	bacon double cheeseburger	*158g*
	BBQ bacon double cheeseburger	*172g*
	McDonald's, bacon and egg McMuffin	*146g*
	Wimpy, bacon in a bun	*105g*
	Wimpy, bacon and egg in a bun	*165g*

Beefburgers	no bun,	
	80% beef, 56g raw, fried or grilled	*36g*
	100% beef, 56g raw, fried or grilled	*34g*
	economy,	
	60% beef, 56g raw, fried or grilled	*40g*
	80% beef, quarterpounder, fried or	
	grilled	*90g*
	100% beef, quarterpounder, fried or	
	grilled	*78g*
	in a bun, average	*105g*
	with cheese, cheeseburger, average	*115g*
	quarterpounder, average	*180g*
	quarter pounder with cheese, average	*200g*
	Burger King,	
	hamburger	*106g*
	cheeseburger	*118g*
	double cheeseburger	*166g*
	cheeseburger deluxe	*147g*
	whopper	*258g*
	double whopper	*334g*
	whopper with cheese	*283g*
	double whopper with cheese	*359g*
	mushroom double Swiss	*168g*

	McDonalds,	
	hamburger	*100g*
	cheeseburger	*117g*
	quarter pounder	*162g*
	quarter pounder with cheese	*195g*
	quarter pounder with cheese deluxe	*220g*
	Big Mac	*204g*
	Wimpy,	
	hamburger	*105g*
	cheeseburger	*120g*
	quarter pounder	*210g*
	quarter pounder with cheese	*225g*
	half pounder	*305g*
	kingsize	*200g*
	leanburger	*235g*
	in batter, average	*130g*
Beef casserole or curry	average portion, small	*180g*
	medium	*260g*
	large	*360g*
Beef, minced	stewed, small, average portion	*100g*
	medium, average portion	*140g*
	large, average portion	*220g*
	stewed with gravy and vegetables,	
	average portion	*270g*
	stewed canned, small	*200g*
	large	*392g*
Beef pies	Beef and onion pastie	*160g*
	Beef and onion pie	*140g*
	Canned steak/steak and kidney pie,	
	small	*213g*
	large	*425g*
	Cornish pastie, mini	*75g*
	medium	*145g*
	large	*227g*
	Scotch pie	*112g*
	Shepherds pie/cottage pie,	
	average portion	*310g*
	Steak and kidney pie individual	*160g*

Meat

	Steak and kidney pudding individual	*141g*
	small	*230g*
	large	*450g*
	Steak and potato pie individual	*128g*
	Steak pie individual	*150g*
	individual, deep filled	*210g*
	Steak pie large, small slice	*90g*
	medium slice	*120g*
	large slice	*150g*
Beef, roast	small, average portion	*50g*
	medium, average portion	*90g*
	large, average portion	*150g*
	thinly sliced beef, 1 slice	*28g*
	thickly sliced beef, 1 slice	*45g*
	1 portion in gravy, purchased frozen	
	beef	*59g*
	gravy	*55g*
Beef, steaks, fried or grilled	small, average portion	*110g*
	medium, average portion	*144g*
	large, average portion	*210g*
	1 fillet steak, 5oz, fried	*108g*
	grilled	*105g*
	8oz fried	*172g*
	grilled	*168g*
	1 minute steak, 5oz, fried	*80g*
	grilled	*78g*
	1 rump steak, 5oz, fried	*103g*
	grilled	*102g*
	8oz, fried	*166g*
	grilled	*163g*
	1 T-bone steak, 8oz, fried	*169g*
	grilled	*166g*
	12oz, fried	*253g*
	grilled	*248g*
Beef, stewed	small average portion	*90g*
	medium average portion	*140g*
	large average portion	*210g*

Beef, stewed with vegetables	small average portion	*230g*
	in gravy, medium average portion	*270g*
	large average portion	*340g*
Black pudding	1 slice	*30g*
	1 portion	*75g*
Bolognese sauce	average portion	*240g*
Braising steak	see beef, stewed	
Burgerbites in baked beans	small tin, beans	*170g*
	burgerbites	*55g*
Cannelloni	average portion	*340g*
	frozen ready meal, serves one	*260g*
Chickbits	in baked beans, small tin, beans	*170g*
	chickbits	*55g*
Chicken in a bun	fried chicken sandwich, chicken only	*70g*
	with bun	*130g*
	Burger King, BK Flamer	*167g*
	Chicken Royale	*224g*
	Kentucky Fried Chicken Sandwich	*174g*
	McDonald's, McChicken Sandwich	*159g*
	Wimpy, Chicken in a bun	*180g*
Chicken breast steak	in breadcrumbs, fried	*100g*
Chicken casserole or curry	small average portion	*180g*
	medium average portion	*260g*
	large average portion	*360g*
Chicken cordon bleu	fried or grilled	*160g*
Chicken fingers	fried, each	*15g*
Chicken Kiev	fried or grilled	*170g*

Meat

Chicken nuggets	pieces, baked or fried, each	*16g*
	6 nuggets average portion	*100g*
	McDonald's 6 McNuggets	*105g*
	Burger King chicken pick 'em ups	
	(for 6)	*111g*
Chicken pie	individual	*130g*
	large	*480g*
	1 slice of large pie, small	*90g*
	medium	*120g*
	large	*150g*
	individual, with mushroom or vegetables	*140g*
Chicken portions	1 breast, no bone, small	*100g*
	medium	*130g*
	large	*150g*
	1 drumstick, with bone	*90g*
	edible portion	*47g*
	1 half, edible portion	*350g*
	1 leg, with bone	*165g*
	edible portion	*90g*
	1 quarter, edible portion	*190g*
	1 thigh, with bone	*75g*
	edible portion	*45g*
	1 wing, with bone	*55g*
	edible portion	*25g*
Chicken portions, fried	1 breast portion, with bone	*70g*
e.g. Kentucky	1 drumstick, with bone	*131g*
	1 rib, with bone	*110g*
	1 thigh, with bone	*107g*
	1 wing, with bone	*73g*
	Hot wings, with bones, 5 pieces	*161g*
Chicken, roast	small average portion	*70g*
	medium average portion	*100g*
	large average portion	*170g*
	in gravy, purchased frozen, chicken	*59g*
	gravy	*55g*
	1 slice roast, breast	*40g*

Meat

Chicken roll	1 slice (diameter 8cm)	*12g*
Chicken sticks	1 fried	*25g*
Chicken tikka and tandoori chicken	see Indian dishes	
Chilli con carne	no rice	*220g*
	purchased frozen ready meal for one	*290g*
	sauce	*155g*
	rice	*135g*
Chinese dishes	beef dishes, e.g. beef in oyster sauce	*360g*
	char-sui buns, steamed, small	*60g*
	large	*112g*
	chicken dishes, e.g. chicken with	
	mushrooms	*400g*
	chop suey dishes, e.g. chicken chop suey	*450g*
	chow mein dishes, e.g. beef chow mein	*350g*
	fu yung dishes, e.g. chicken fu yung	*310g*
	pancake roll, small	*90g*
	large	*140g*
	spare ribs in sauce	*340g*
	spring roll, meat, average	*55g*
	sweet and sour dishes, e.g. sweet and	
	sour pork	*300g*
	pork balls only	*150g*
	vegetable dishes, fried, from takeaway	*340g*
Chopped ham and pork	thinly sliced, 1 slice	*14g*
Corned beef	1 slice, thin	*38g*
	thick	*50g*
	1 small can	*198g*
Cornish pastie	medium	*155g*
	large	*260g*
Cottage pie/Shepherds pie	average portion	*310g*

Meat

Curries	average, e.g. Bhuna, Dhansak, Dupiaza, Kashmir, Korma, Madras, Malaya, Patia, Rogan Josh, Vindaloo	*350g*
	(see also Indian dishes)	
	frozen purchased ready meal with rice	*290g*
Duck	breast and wing, roast, meat and skin only	*185g*
	crispy duck, average takeaway portion	*125g*
Faggots	in gravy, two	*150g*
Fillet steak	average, 5oz, fried	*108g*
	grilled	*105g*
Game	1 grouse, with bone	*350g*
	meat only	*160g*
	1 partridge, with bone	*550g*
	meat only	*260g*
	1 pheasant, with bone	*800g*
	meat only	*430g*
	1 pigeon, with bone	*240g*
	meat only	*115g*
	1 rabbit, with bone	*850g*
	meat only	*510g*
	venison, average portion	*120g*
Game pie	average slice	*175g*
Garlic sausage	1 small average slice (diameter 5cm)	*5g*
	1 large average slice (diameter 11cm)	*12g*
Ham	average slice	*23g*
	very thinly sliced ham, 1 slice	*11g*
	canned ham, average slice, thin	*35g*
	thick	*45g*
	honey glazed ham, average slice	*28g*
	thin slice	*17g*
	parma ham, average slice	*17g*
	average portion	*47g*

Hamburgers	see beefburgers	
Hashbrown	McDonald's	*51g*
Haslet	average slice	*14g*
Heart	lambs, 1 whole cooked	*200g*
Indian dishes	Biriani, rice and meat	*400g*
	biriani sauce	*200g*
	Chicken tikka, as starter	*120g*
	Chicken tikka, as main course	*200g*
	Chicken tikka mossala	*300g*
	curry, e.g. Bhuna, Dhansak, Dupiaza, Kashmir, Korma, Madras, Malaya, Patia, Rogan Josh, Vindaloo	*350g*
	Kebab, rashmi, seesh, shami, as starter	*140g*
	Meat tikka, main course	*200g*
	Samosa, meat, small	*40g*
	medium	*70g*
	large	*120g*
	Tandoori chicken, as starter	*100g*
	Tandoori chicken, main course,	
	half chicken	*700g*
	edible portion	*350g*
	whole chicken	*1400g*
	edible portion	*700g*
Irish stew	average portion	*330g*
	canned, 1 large can	*425g*
Kebab	average portion meat on skewer	*90g*
	Doner kebab, small, meat	*85g*
	pitta bread	*75g*
	salad	*70g*
	Doner kebab, large, meat	*130g*
	pitta bread	*95g*
	salad	*90g*
	Kofte kebab, meat only	*90g*
	Rashmi, Seesh, Shami kebab, Indian starter	*140g*

Meat

	Shish kebab, meat on skewer, meat only	85g
Kidney	in gravy, average portion	112g
	in individual steak and kidney pie	15g
	1 tablespoon cooked kidney	40g
	1 whole lamb's kidney, fried	35g
	1 whole pig's kidney	140g
Lamb casserole or curry	small average portion	180g
	medium average portion	260g
	large average portion	360g
Lamb chop	average braising chop, with bone	120g
	edible portion only	70g
	average chump chop, with bone, fried or grilled	120g
	edible portion only	70g
	average cutlet, with bone, fried or grilled	98g
	edible portion only	50g
Lamb, roast	small average portion	50g
	medium average portion	90g
	large average portion	150g
	average slice	30g
Lasagne	average portion	420g
	purchased frozen ready meal for one	290g
Liver	1 slice lamb's/calf's, fried or grilled	40g
	1 slice pig's/ox, fried or grilled	50g
	1 portion fried or grilled	100g
	1 portion, in gravy, liver only	70g
	1 portion, with onions in gravy, purchased frozen	142g
Luncheon meat	average slice	14g
	thick slice	20g
Meat dishes	average portions	
	Cannelloni	340g
	Chicken chow mein	300g
	Chilli con carne, no rice	220g

	Hot-pots	*260g*
	Irish stew	*260g*
	Lasagne	*420g*
	Meatballs, 6 meat balls, canned	*80g*
	Moussaka	*330g*
	Shepherds pie, Cottage pie	*310g*
	Spaghetti bolognese, sauce only	*240g*
	stews, casseroles, average	*260g*
	Tacos, 1 filled shell, meat only	*65g*
	taco shell	*14g*
Minute steak	average fried	*80g*
	grilled	*78g*
Partridge	see game	
Pastie	see cornish pastie, beef pies	
Pâté	average portion as starter	*80g*
	average on slice of bread	*40g*
Pheasant	see game	
Pies	see beef pies, chicken pies, pork pies, sausage rolls	
Pigeon	see game	
Pork casserole or curry	average portion, small	*180g*
	medium	*260g*
	large	*360g*
Pork chops	chump chops, no bone fried or grilled	*170g*
	lean pork escalope, fried or grilled	*75g*
	loin steaks, no bone, fried or grilled	*120g*
	rib end chops, with bone, fried or grilled	*165g*
	edible portion	*85g*
	shoulder steak, no bone, fried or grilled	*135g*
	spare rib chops, with bone, fried or grilled	*220g*
	edible portion	*140g*

	streaky slices, with bone, fried or grilled	*170g*
	edible portion	*110g*
	other pork chops, average, with bone,	
	fried or grilled	*150g*
	edible portion	*75g*

Pork luncheon meat	thinly sliced, 1 slice	*14g*

Pork pies	buffet pie	*75g*
	individual pie	*140g*
	large/family pie	*450g*
	mini pie	*50g*
	slice pie	*60g*
	slice Grosvenor pork pie	*113g*
	veal and ham pie, 1 slice	*140g*

Pork, roast	small average portion	*50g*
	medium average portion	*90g*
	large average portion	*150g*
	average slice	*40g*
	thinly sliced pork, 1 slice	*28g*

Rabbit	see game	

Ravioli	see Pasta, rice and grains	

Rump steak	average, 5oz, fried	*103g*
	grilled	*102g*

Salami	1 small average slice (diameter 5cm)	*5g*
	1 large average slice (diameter 11cm)	*12g*
	1 snack salami (peperami)	*25g*

Sausage rolls	1 sausage roll, small	*32g*
	medium	*60g*
	large/jumbo	*145g*
	1 'mini cocktail' sausage roll	*14g*

Sausages	1 chipolata, fried or grilled	*20g*
	1 Chorizos snack sausage	*30g*
	1 cocktail sausage fried or grilled	*10g*
	1 German sausage, bratwurst	*75g*

Meat

	1 hot dog sausage/frankfurter, small	*23g*
	large	*47g*
	1 kabanos sausage, snack	*30g*
	McDonald's Sausage and Egg McMuffin	*171g*
	1 Peperami	*25g*
	1 pork/beef, buffet, fried or grilled	*12g*
	1 pork/beef, large fried or grilled	*40g*
	1 pork/beef, thin, fried or grilled	*20g*
	1 saveloy	*65g*
	sausage in batter	*115g*
	Wimpy Bender (frankfurter) in a bun	*140g*
Scotch eggs	see Egg and egg dishes	
Scotch pie	individual	*112g*
Shepherds pie	cottage pie, average portion	*310g*
	purchased frozen ready meal for one	*210g*
Spam	1 average slice	*14g*
	fritter	*30g*
Spare rib chops	with bone, fried or grilled	*220g*
	edible portion	*140g*
Spare ribs	1 rack, 4 ribs, with bone	*120g*
	edible portion	*60g*
	average portion, no bone	*120g*
	Chinese spare ribs in sauce	*340g*
	Kentucky, spare ribs with bone	*224g*
	spare ribs in full house, with bone	*112g*
	1 Ungers King Rib	*60g*
Spring roll	see Meat and Vegetable sections	
Steak	see beef	
Steak and kidney pies	see beef pies	
Steak and kidney puddings	see beef pies	

Stewing steak	see beef stewed	
Tandoori chicken	see Indian dishes	
T-bone steak	average, 8oz, fried	*169g*
	grilled	*166g*
Tongue	1 average slice	*25g*
Tripe	1 average portion, stewed	*150g*
Turkey breast roll	thinly sliced, 1 slice	*11g*
Turkey burger	1 breaded and fried	*90g*
Turkey, roast	small average portion	*70g*
	medium average portion	*90g*
	large average portion	*140g*
	thinly sliced, 1 slice	*23g*
	1 average steak	*100g*
Turkey roll	1 slice	*19g*
Veal and ham pie	1 slice	*140g*
Veal, cutlet/escalope	in breadcrumbs, fried	*150g*
Venison	1 average portion	*120g*

MILK AND CREAM

Milk and cream

Milk	1 pint	*585g*
	½ pint	*293g*
	⅓ pint	*195g*
	¼ pint	*146g*
	⅛ pint	*73g*
	1 tablespoon	*15g*
	1 dessertspoon	*10g*
	1 teaspoon	*5g*
	whole, in 1 cup tea/coffee	*25g*
	in 1 mug tea/coffee	*30g*
	semi-skimmed, in 1 cup tea/coffee	*30g*
	in 1 mug tea/coffee	*40g*
	skimmed, in 1 cup tea/coffee	*35g*
	in 1 mug tea/coffee	*50g*
	average glass	*200g*
	with cereals, average portion	*100g*
	canned, semi-skimmed, ready to drink	*300g*
	dried milk, 1 teaspoon	*3g*
	evaporated, 1 small can	*170g*
	individual portion pack for tea	*15g*
Coffee whitener powder	1 teaspoon	*3g*
	1 heaped teaspoon	*4.5g*
	1 sachet, Coffee-mate	*3g*
	1 heaped teaspoon, Coffee-mate Lite	*4.5g*
Cream	1 small carton (5 fl. oz)	*150g*
	1 large carton (10 fl. oz)	*300g*
	1 tablespoon, single	*15g*
	1 tablespoon, double, whipped	*30g*
	1 tablespoon, aerosol cream	*10g*
	individual portion pack for coffee	*15g*
	fresh cream whipped on fruit or cake	*45g*
	aerosol cream on fruit or cake	*17g*
Dream Topping	on fruit or cake	*15g*
Dried milk	1 teaspoon	*3g*

Milk & Cream

Flavoured milk	Aero chocolate drinks	*192g*
	Crazy Milk, individual carton	*214g*
	bottle (500 mls)	*544g*
	Mars bar milk (200 ml)	*227g*
	Nesquik semi-skimmed	*190g*
Milkshake	McDonald's	*300g*
Super whip	average portion	*38g*
Tip Top dessert topping	3 dessertspoons	*50g*
Yoghurt drinks	see Yoghurt section	

MISCELLANEOUS

Baking powder	1 level teaspoon	*4g*
Bovril	see Marmite	
Cherry	glacé or maraschino, 1	*5g*
Complan	1 sachet	*57g*
Curry powder	1 level teaspoon	*3g*
Glacé cherry	1	*5g*
Gravy browning	1 teaspoon	*5g*
Herbs	dried, 1 teaspoon	*1g*
Hundreds and thousands	1 teaspoon	*4g*
Maraschino cherry	1	*5g*
Marmite, Bovril	thin scraping on bread	*1g*
	thick scraping on bread	*4g*
	1 heaped teaspoon	*18g*
	1 level teaspoon	*9g*
Mustard	1 level teaspoon	*8g*
	powder, 1 level teaspoon	*3g*
Oxo	stock cube, 1	*7g*
Parsley	dried, 1 level teaspoon	*1g*
	fresh, 1 large sprig	*1g*
Pepper	1 level teaspoon	*2g*
Salt	1 level teaspoon	*5g*
	1 heaped teaspoon	*8g*
Spices	dried, 1 teaspoon	*3g*

| **Stock cube** | Knorr, 1 | *9g* |
| | Oxo, 1 | *6g* |

| **Stuffing** | 1 portion | *50g* |

| **Vinegar** | 1 teaspoon | *5g* |
| | 1 tablespoon | *15g* |

| **Yeast extract** | see Marmite | |

NUTS AND SEEDS

Almonds	6 whole	*13g*
Brazil nuts	3 whole	*10g*
Cashew nuts	10 whole	*10g*
	roasted, salted, per bag	*25g/50g/100g*
Chestnuts	5 whole, peeled	*50g*
Cob nuts	hazelnuts, 10 whole	*10g*
Macadamia nuts	6, no shell	*10g*
Mixed nuts and raisins	per bag, Golden Wonder	*40g*
	per bag, Big D, KP, Percy Dalton	*50g*
Monkey nuts	1 with shell	*2g*
Peanuts	10 whole	*13g*
	roasted, salted, per bag, small	*25g*
	medium	*50g*
	large	*100g*
	dry roasted, per bag	*50g/100g*
	steam nuts, per bag	*45g*
Peanut butter	thickly spread on one slice	*20g*
	thinly spread on one slice	*12g*
	1 portion pack	*25g*
Peanuts and raisins	1 handful	*40g*
Pecan nut	1, no shell	*6g*
Pistachio nuts	10, kernels only	*10g*
Popcorn	caramel coated	*25g/75g*
Sesame seeds	1 tablespoon	*12g*

Nuts & Seeds

Sesame seed spread	Tahini, 1 heaped teaspoon	*19g*
Sunflower seeds	1 tablespoon	*16g*
Tahini	1 heaped teaspoon	*19g*
Walnuts	6 halves	*20g*

PASTA, RICE AND GRAINS

Barley, pearl	boiled, 1 tablespoon	*20g*
	1 tablespoon dried, after boiling	*60g*
Bran	1 tablespoon	*7g*
Cornflour	1 heaped tablespoon	*30g*
Cous-cous	cracked wheat, average portion	*150g*
	1 tablespoon	*33g*
Custard powder	1 heaped tablespoon	*30g*
Dumpling, suet	1 average	*70g*
Flour	any, 1 level tablespoon	*20g*
	1 heaped tablespoon	*30g*
Lasagne	see Meat	
Macaroni	boiled, small average portion	*150g*
	medium	*230g*
	large	*350g*
	1 tablespoon	*30g*
Macaroni cheese	average portion	*220g*
	canned, average portion	*210g*
	large can	*430g*
	small can	*210g*
	purchased frozen ready meal for one	*280g*
Noodles	instant, 1 packet, made up	*280g*
Oats	1 tablespoon	*15g*
	1 tablespoon jumbo oats	*10g*
Pasta	cooked, small average portion	*150g*
	medium average portion	*230g*
	large average portion	*350g*

	canned in tomato sauce, side dish	
	average portion	*125g*
	large can	*425g*
	small can	*215g*
	1 tablespoon	*30g*
	purchased ready meal, for one	*235g*
	salad, can	*210g*
Pot-noodles	as served	*300g*
Ravioli	average portion	*250g*
	canned, average portion	*220g*
	large can	*440g*
	small can	*215g*
	1 tablespoon	*45g*
Rice	boiled, average portion, small	*100g*
	medium	*180g*
	large	*290g*
	1 heaped tablespoon	*40g*
	boiled/fried, take-away portion	*300g*
	pilau (fried) rice, average portion	*180g*
	salad, 1 tablespoon	*45g*
	savoury, average portion	*180g*
	1 packet made up	*300g*
Sago, semolina, tapioca pudding	average portion	*200g*
	canned, small can	*210g*
	large can	*430g*
Spaghetti	boiled, small average portion	*150g*
	medium average portion	*220g*
	large average portion	*270g*
Spaghetti Bolognaise	average portion	*470g*
	restaurant portion	*400g*
	pasta	*230g*
	sauce	*170g*
	canned, large can	*430g*
	small can	*210g*
	purchased frozen ready meal for one	*320g*

	pasta	*100g*
	sauce	*220g*
Tortellini	average portion	*320g*
	canned, 1 tablespoon	*50g*
Wheatgerm	1 tablespoon	*5g*
Yorkshire pudding	average portion	*80g*

PUDDINGS, CHILLED DESSERTS AND FRUIT PIES

Apple charlotte	average portion	*170g*
Apple crumble	(or any fruit) average portion	*170g*
Apple Danish	Burger King	*100g*
Apple pie	see Fruit pie	
	deep fried, Burger King	*115g*
	deep fried, Kentucky	*78g*
	deep fried, McDonald's	*81g*
Arctic roll	average slice, one fifth	*50g*
Bavarois	purchased, Nestlé	*100g*
Blancmange	average portion	*150g*
Bread and butter pudding	average portion	*170g*
Bread pudding	average slice	*190g*
Caramel surprise	St Ivel	*128g*
Cheesecake	average slice	*120g*
	individual	*90g*
Chocolate desserts	Cadbury's Bournville dessert	*80g*
	Cadbury's Dairy milk	*80g*
	Chocoholics	*110g*
	Chocolate Surprise, St Ivel	*128g*
	Hippo Mud	*125g*
	Milky Bar (white chocolate)	*90g*
	Nesquik	*80g*
	Rolo	*70g*
	Yopi, Yoplait	*100g*
Christmas pudding	average portion	*100g*

Creme caramel		90g
	purchased, La Laitière	100g
	purchased, St Ivel	128g
Crumble	any fruit, average portion	170g
Custard	average portion	120g
	canned, half a can	210g
	cartoned, half a carton	265g
	ready to serve, per individual pot	150g
Egg custard	average portion	110g
Fruit fool	average portion	120g
	individual, purchased	115g
Fruit pie	average portion	110g
	deep fried, average portion	80g
	individual, small	54g
	individual, large	100g
	half large purchased pie	150g
Fruit sponge	average portion	110g
Fruit sundae	ice cream, fruit, sauce and cream	180g
Fruit tart/flan	average portion	95g
Instant whip/Angel Delight	average portion	120g
	purchased, ready to eat, per pot	100g
Jelly	average portion	115g
	purchased, ready to eat, per pot	125g
Lemon meringue pie	average portion	95g
Milk jelly	Chambourcy Disney	125g
Milk puddings	average portion	200g
	canned, large	425g
	small	213g

	Ambrosia, per pot	*150g*
	Müllerrice, per pot	*200g*
Mousse	purchased frozen, individual, average	*74g*
	purchased, individual, average	*60g*
	Aero milk chocolate	*62g*
	Chambourcy Disney, Chocolate	*62g*
	Delight reduced fat chocolate	*70g*
	Hippo Pota Mousse	*62g*
	Real Chocolate	*63g*
	St Ivel, Cadbury's Dairy Milk	*62g*
Pancakes (crêpes)	small	*60g*
	medium	*110g*
	large	*150g*
	filled with fruit, average portion	*145g*
Pavlova	average portion	*100g*
Profiteroles	with chocolate sauce and cream	*155g*
Rice pudding	see Milk puddings	
Sorbet	average portion	*95g*
Soufflé	average portion	*113g*
Sponge pudding	average portion	*110g*
	canned, whole	*300g*
	purchased, individual	*100g*
Suet pudding	average pudding	*90g*
Tiramisu	purchased, individual	*90g*
Trifle	Cadbury's Dairy Milk Chocolate	*105g*
	homemade	*170g*
	individual purchased	*113g*
Viennetta	average slice	*56g*

Waffle, sweet		*65g*
General puddings	small	*120g*
	medium	*150g*
	large	*180g*

Puddings

SANDWICHES AND BAPS (PURCHASED)

Many of the large supermarket chains are now selling pre-packed sandwiches. Although the quantities of ingredients used will be very variable, typical weights of 1 round (i.e., 2 slices of medium sliced bread) of the more popular types of sandwiches are presented below.

Sandwiches

Beef, roast & salad	*165g*
Cheese & pickle	*185g*
Chicken, roast & salad	*205g*
Egg mayonnaise & cress	*145g*
Ham, cheese & pickle	*180g*
Tuna mayonnaise	*165g*

Baps

Cheese & pickle	*195g*
Chicken salad	*190g*

SAUCES, PICKLES AND SOUPS

Apple sauce	average portion	*20g*
Blue cheese dressing	1 tablespoon	*25g*
Bread sauce	average portion	*45g*
Brown sauce	1 sachet	*12g*
	1 portion pack	*20g*
Cheese sauce	with meat/fish/vegetables,	
	small portion	*30g*
	medium portion	*62g*
	large portion	*90g*
Chutney, mango	1 teaspoon	*10g*
	1 tablespoon	*33g*
Cranberry sauce	average portion	*30g*
Curry sauce	average portion	*150g*
French dressing	1 salad, average portion	*15g*
	1 tablespoon	*15g*
Gravy	small average portion	*25g*
	medium average portion	*50g*
	large average portion	*120g*
Horseradish sauce	1 sachet	*12g*
	1 portion pack	*20g*
Mayonnaise	with salad, average portion	*30g*
	1 heaped tablespoon	*33g*
	1 level tablespoon	*15g*
	1 portion pack	*12g*
Mint jelly	average portion	*20g*

Sauces & Pickles

Mint sauce	average portion	*10g*
	1 teaspoon	*7g*
Mustard	average portion, smooth type	*2g*
	1 sachet	*5g*
	average portion, whole grain type	*14g*
Onion sauce	average portion	*62g*
Parsley sauce	average portion	*62g*
Pesto	1 tablespoon	*26g*
Pickle	with ploughman's, average portion	*40g*
	1 heaped teaspoon	*15g*
	1 tablespoon	*40g*
	1 portion pack	*20g*
Pickled beetroot	1 average	*35g*
Pickled cabbage	1 tablespoon	*45g*
Pickled gherkin	1 small	*8g*
	1 medium	*25g*
	1 large, pickled cucumber	*60g*
Pickled onion	1 average	*15g*
	1 large	*25g*
	1 silverskin onion	*2g*
Prawn cocktail sauce	average	*40g*
Redcurrant jelly	1 teaspoon	*9g*
Relish	in burger	*15g*
	1 heaped teaspoon	*15g*
Salad cream	average with salad	*20g*
	1 sachet	*12g*
Savoury sauces	see white sauce	

Soup	small average portion	*150g*
	medium average portion	*220g*
	large average portion	*300g*
	main course soup	*260g*
	starter soup	*190g*
	cup-a-soup, made up	*215g*
	large can	*405g*
	small can	*300g*
	vending machine soup	*170g*
Soy sauce	1 teaspoon	*5g*
Sweet 'n' sour sauce	average portion	*150g*
	Burger King	*25g*
	McDonalds	*32g*
Tartare sauce	average serving	*30g*
	1 sachet	*12g*
Thousand island dressing	1 tablespoon	*30g*
Tomato ketchup	1 sachet	*12g*
	1 portion pack	*20g*
Tomato sauce	average, with meat/fish/pasta	*90g*
White sauce	with meat/fish/vegetables, small	*30g*
	medium	*62g*
	large	*90g*

SAVOURY SNACKS
All weights given per bag

Apple Crackles		*20g*
Bacon Fries		*25g/50g*
Bensons Crinkle Cut		*33g*
Bombay mix	Sharwoods	*100g*
	Golden Glow	*28g*
	Percy Dalton	*30g*
Brannigans		*37g*
Californian corn chips		*100g*
Cheeky Chicken		*18g*
Cheese Quavers		*20g*
Cheese Savouries		*33g*
Cheese Snips		*30g*
Cheeselets		*25g*
Crinkles		*40g*
Crisps	small	*25/27/28/30g*
	medium/maxi	*40g*
	large	*75g*
	family pack	*100g*
	1 large crisp	*2g*
Dinobites		*18g*
Discos		*18g/29g*
Farmhouse jackets		*40g*

Frazzles		*27g*
Frisps		*28g*
Garlic mini breads		*28g*
Golden lights		*25g*
Good 'n' Crunchy Crisps		*35g*
Groovers		*30g*
Horizons		*50g*
Hula Hoops		*30g*
Jack Spratt's lower fat snacks		*35g*
Jackets		*28g*
Japanese Rice Crackers		*56g*
Jumbo Jaws		*26g*
Kettle Chips		*50g/100g*
Krunchie Puffs	cheese	*9g*
	salt & vinegar	*10g*
Krunchie Onion Rings	salt & vinegar	*9g*
Krunchie Sticks		*19g*
McCoys Cracker Snacks		*40g*
Mean Beans		*21g*
Mexican Chips		*30g*
Mignons Morceau		*125g*

Monster Munch		*27g*
Nik Naks		*35g*
Oatsters		*28g/50g*
Odduns		*26g*
On Yums	pickled onion	*18g*
Onion Rings		*50g*
Petrified Prawn		*18g*
Pork Crackles		*24g*
Pork Scratchings		*22g*
Prawn Crackers		*30g/40g*
	Chinese take-away	*70g*
Pringles	Original, per tube	*200g*
Quarterbacks	cheese burger, burger pickle	*20g*
Quavers		*20g*
Real McCoys		*40g*
Ringos		*24g*
Ritz Sandwich	pack of 4	*33g*
Roysters		*28g*
Ruffles		*28g*
Savoury Huggy Bears		*25g*
Savoury Moments		*28g/50g*

Scampi Fries		*27g*
Skips		*18g*
Space Raiders		*19g*
Spicy Popadums		*30g*
Solos		*25g*
Square Crisps		*25g*
Stackers		*100g*
Supa Krunchie Onion Rings	fried onion	*18g*
Supa Krunchies		*22g*
Supa Krunchies	cheese & tomato	*18g*
	salt & vinegar	*19g*
Taco	1 shell	*10g*
Tangy Toms		*9g/18g*
Thunder Cats		*18g*
Tortilla Chips		*50g/100g*
Transform-A-snack		*20g*
Tubaloops		*20g*
Twiglets		*25g/50g/100g*
Wheatcrunchies		*35g*
Whickettes		*50g*
Wotsits		*25g*

Savoury snacks

SUGARS, PRESERVES AND SWEET SAUCES

Brandy butter	average portion	*30g*
Brandy sauce, rum sauce	average portion	*60g*
Cherry	glacé or maraschino, 1	*5g*
Chocolate sauce	average portion	*60g*
Chocolate spread	1 average spreading on 1 slice of bread	*20g*
	1 heaped teaspoon	*16g*
	1 level teaspoon	*8g*
Custard	See Puddings, chilled desserts and fruit pies	
Honey	1 average spreading on 1 slice of bread	*20g*
	1 heaped teaspoon	*17g*
	1 level teaspoon	*8g*
	1 portion pack	*28g*
Ice-cream topping sauce	average topping	*28g*
Jam, marmalade, lemon curd	1 average spreading on 1 slice of bread	*15g*
	1 heaped teaspoon	*18g*
	1 level teaspoon	*8g*
	1 individual carton	*20g*
	1 mini glass jar	*28g/43g*
Maple syrup	serving on waffles	*55g*
Marmalade	see jam	
Sugar	1 cube	*5g*
	1 heaped teaspoon	*6g*
	1 level teaspoon	*4g*
	1 'packet' sugar	*6g*
	1 tablespoon	*20g*

VEGETABLES

Artichoke	one globe heart, edible portion	*50g*
Asparagus	5 spears	*125g*
Aubergine	half including skin, cooked	*130g*
Baked beans	in tomato sauce, small portion	*80g*
	medium portion	*135g*
	large portion	*190g*
	1 small can	*150g/205g*
	1 large can	*420g*
	1 tablespoon	*40g*
	with sausage, small can, beans	*170g*
	sausage	*55g*
	large can, beans	*305g*
	sausage	*145g*
	with burgerbites, chickbits, small can,	
	beans	*170g*
	burgerbites/chickbits	*55g*
Beanburger	Burger King, with bun	*240g*
	Wimpy, with bun	*235g*
Beans	broad, 2 tablespoons	*120g*
	french, small portion	*60g*
	medium portion	*90g*
	large portion	*120g*
	dried, boiled, 2 tablespoons	*60g*
	red kidney, 1 heaped tablespoon	
	cooked beans	*35g*
	runner, small portion	*60g*
	medium portion	*90g*
	large portion	*120g*
Beansprouts	1 tablespoon	*20g*
Beetroot	1 small whole	*35g*
	per slice	*10g*
	average portion	*40g*

Bhindi	see okra	
Broccoli spears/calabrese	1 spear, boiled	*45g*
	boiled, small portion	*60g*
	medium portion	*85g*
	large portion	*110g*
Brussels sprouts	average serving, 9 sprouts	*90g*
	small portion	*60g*
	medium portion	*90g*
	large portion	*120g*
Bubble and squeak	fried, average portion	*200g*
Cabbage, boiled	any, small portion	*60g*
	medium portion	*95g*
	large portion	*120g*
	red/white, raw, ⅙ small cabbage	*90g*
Calabrese	1 spear, boiled	*45g*
Carrots	boiled, small portion	*40g*
	medium portion	*60g*
	large portion	*85g*
	canned, 1 medium carrot	*12g*
	1 small, boiled	*30g*
	1 medium, boiled	*80g*
	1 large, boiled	*140g*
	a few slices	*20g*
	1 tablespoon	*40g*
Cauliflower	1 floret	*10g*
	boiled, small portion	*60g*
	boiled, medium portion	*90g*
	boiled, large portion	*120g*
	Bhaji	*140g*
	cauliflower cheese, see Cheese dishes	
Celery	1 stick	*30g*
	boiled, small portion	*30g*
	medium portion	*50g*
	large portion	*80g*

Vegetables

Chick peas	1 heaped tablespoon cooked peas	*35g*
	2–3 tablespoons, cooked	*90g*
	paste, hummous, 1 tablespoon	*30g*
	average portion	*60g*
	chick pea curry, from takeaway	*210g*
Chinese leaves	1 large leaf	*40g*
Chips	see potato chips	
Coleslaw	1 tablespoon	*45g*
	1 small tub	*120g*
	1 large tub	*250g*
	take-away portion, Kentucky	*100g*
	1 can	*210g*
Corn-on-the-cob	see sweetcorn	
Courgettes	1 medium cooked	*100g*
	1 large cooked	*150g*
	small portion	*60g*
	medium portion	*90g*
	large portion	*120g*
Cress	see mustard and cress	
Cucumber	1 slice	*6g*
	1″ piece	*60g*
	average in salad	*23g*
French fries	see potato chips	
Green banana	1 whole boiled	*140g*
Leeks	1 medium, boiled	*160g*
	stem, white portion only	*80g*
	average serving	*75g*
Lentils	boiled, 1 tablespoon	*40g*
	boiled (2oz raw)	*120g*

Lettuce	4 small leaves	20g
	round, average serving in salad	30g
	iceberg, average serving in salad	80g
Marrow	average serving	65g
Mixed bean salad	small can	210g
	1 tablespoon	30g
Mixed vegetables	average serving	90g
Mushrooms	button, raw, 1 small	5g
	1 medium	10g
	1 large	20g
	breaded, average serving	110g
	fried, average serving	44g
	stewed, average serving	56g
Mustard and cress	1 tablespoon	5g
	in sandwich	2g
	quarter of a punnet	10g
Okra	ladies fingers, bhindi, 1 medium	5g
	bhindi bhaji, okra curry	250g
Onion	raw, 1 small	60g
	1 medium	150g
	1 large	240g
	1 slice	20g
	bhaji, fried, 1 average	35g
	boiled, average serving	60g
	fried, average serving	40g
	pickled, 1 average	15g
	1 large	25g
	rings, battered, average portion	100g
	spring, 1	10g
Parsnips	average portion, small	40g
	medium	65g
	large	85g

Vegetables

	1 tablespoon	*50g*
	1 medium baked	*90g*
Peas	average portion, small	*40g*
	medium	*70g*
	large	*100g*
	1 tablespoon	*30g*
	mushy, average portion	*80g*
	mushy, fish and chip shop, average portion	*125g*
	canned, 1 tablespoon	*30g*
Pepper	green or red, 1 medium	*160g*
	sliced, 1 ring	*10g*
	half a stuffed pepper	*175g*
Plantain	1 whole, boiled	*200g*
Potatoes	baked, jacket, small with skin	*100g*
	without skin	*88g*
	medium, with skin	*180g*
	without skin	*160g*
	large, with skin	*220g*
	without skin	*195g*
	boiled, 1 average old potato	*60g*
	1 average new potato	*40g*
	1 average portion, small	*120g*
	medium	*175g*
	large	*220g*
	cakes, fried, each	*80g*
	chips, 1 chip	*10g*
	chips, average portion, small	*100g*
	medium	*165g*
	large	*240g*
	average portion, fish and chip shop chips	*210g*
	average portion 'french fries'	*110g*
	Burger King, small	*75g*
	regular	*116g*
	large	*142g*

Kentucky, french fries, regular		*130g*
	large	*165g*
McDonald's, french fries, regular		*77g*
	medium	*110g*
	large	*155g*
Wimpy, french fries		*110g*
crisps, see Savoury snacks		
croquette, fried, 1 average		*90g*
grilled, 1 average		*80g*
crunchies, fried, 1		*9g*
grilled, 1		*6g*
average portion		*90g*
duchesse, 1		*30g*
fritter, 1		*120g*
hashbrowns, Burger King (6)		*58g*
mashed, portions as boiled		
1 tablespoon		*45g*
1 scoop		*60g*
1 forkful		*30g*
pancakes, baked/grilled		*50g*
fried		*56g*
roast, 1 small potato		*50g*
1 medium potato		*85g*
1 large potato		*130g*
average portion		*200g*
salad, 1 tablespoon		*45g*
1 average portion		*85g*
1 tub		*250g*
1 can		*210g/440g*
sauté, average portion		*100g*
scallops, average portion		*150g*
waffles, 1 grilled		*45g*

Radish	1 average	*8g*
Ratatouille	1 tablespoon	*30g*
	average serving	*180g*
Salads, various	1 tub	*200g/250g*
Sauerkraut	1 tablespoon	*30g*

Spinach	average serving	*90g*
	1 tablespoon	*40g*
Spring onion	1 average	*10g*
Spring roll	average, fried	*60g*
Swede	boiled, small portion	*40g*
	medium portion	*60g*
	large portion	*85g*
Sweet potatoes	boiled, 2 medium	*130g*
Sweetcorn	kernels only, 1 tablespoon	*30g*
	average portion	*85g*
	1 corn-on-the-cob, kernels only	*125g*
	fritter, 1	*85g*
Tomato	1 small	*65g*
	1 medium	*85g*
	1 large, e.g. beefsteak tomato	*150g*
	1 slice	*17g*
	1 cherry tomato	*15g*
	average in salad	*34g*
	peeled tomatoes, large can	*400g*
Turnip	boiled, see swede	
	1 whole boiled	*110g*
Vegeburger	average, fried	*56g*
Vegetable casserole/stew	small average portion	*180g*
	medium average portion	*260g*
	large average portion	*360g*
Vegetable curry	1 serving, 3–4 tablespoons	*200g*
Vegetable pastie		*155g*
Vegetable salad	in mayonnaise, 1 tablespoon	*45g*
	can	*210g/440g*

Vegetable samosa	1 average, purchased	*75g*
	average portion (2)	*100g*
Vegetable spring roll	average	*60g*
Watercress	quarter of a bunch	*20g*
Yam	boiled, size of a medium potato	*130g*

Vegetables

YOGHURTS AND FROMAGE FRAIS

Yoghurt

1 tablespoon low fat	*40g*
1 tablespoon thick/Greek	*45g*

Yoghurt is generally purchased in cartons of 125g or 150g. Examples of some common brands in each category are listed below:

125g pots

Boots Shapers, fruit
Chambourcy Disney, fruit
Chambourcy Disney, set
Country Love, thick & creamy fruit
Danone Bio
Danone Bio—fruit on the bottom
Danone Bio Lite
Eden Vale, French style
Kool live, real fruit set
Marks & Spencer Bio
Munch Bunch, real fruit
Munch Bunch, set
Own brand, diet, very low fat, fruit
Own brand, low fat, French set
St Ivel Shape, French Style set
St Ivel, low fat
St Ivel, Fiendish Faces
St Ivel, Shape, low fat fruit
St Ivel Real
Safeway Bio layer, low fat
Sainsburys Bio, wholegrain fruit
Sainsburys Diet Bio natural
Sainsburys Mr Men, 'no bits'
Sainsburys wholemilk, organic
Ski Bio
Ski Diet
Thunderbirds, low fat

150g pots

Eden Vale, natural
La Laitière, whole milk, fruit (bottles)

Marks & Spencer Lite, very low fat
Marks & Spencer, mild & thick, low fat,
   high fruit
Own brand, Bio
Own brand, Bio, diet
Own brand, low fat, fruit
Own brand, thick & creamy, fruit
Safeway, rich & creamy
Ski, extra fruit
Ski, fruit

Other fruit yoghurts	Boots, low fat	*170g*
	Cuisine light	*175g*
	Dairy Fresh, real fruit, low fat	*115g*
	Loseley	*140g*
	Müller light	*200g*
Baby yoghurts	Cow & Gate (jar)	*150g*
	St Ivel Baby & Toddler	*90g*
Custard style yoghurts	Boots	*150g*
	Boots, low fat	*170g*
	Safeway	*125g*
	Sainsburys	*125g*
	Somerfield	*150g*
	Tesco	*125g*
	Waitrose	*150g*
Frozen yoghurt	Average portion	*56g*
	Boots frozen yoghurt in tubs	*100g*
Greek yoghurt	Marks & Spencer Greek Style	*125g*
	Own brand, Greek style, diet fruit/fruit/ natural	*150g*
	Total Greek	*200g/500g*
Pasteurised fruit yoghurts	Dairy Crest	*125g*
	Fruit Basket	*250g*
	Fruittis	*125g*
	St Ivel Prize	*125g*

Sheeps milk yoghurt	Woodlands Park, fruit	142g
	Woodlands Park, natural	227g
Split yoghurts	Boots Bio Split—yoghurt	140g
	—fruit	35g
	Cuisine Chocolate Crunch—yoghurt	130g
	—biscuit	20g
	Marks & Spencer Lite, yoghurt and fruit	150g
	Marks & Spencer Swiss style, yoghurt and fruit	175g
	Marks & Spencer Swiss style yoghurt and muesli	150g
	Müller Crunch Corner—banana yoghurt	135g
	—chocoflakes	15g
	Müller Crunch Corner—wholemilk yoghurt	150g
	—cereal, nuts and raisins	25g
	Müller Crunch Corner—wholemilk yoghurt	150g
	—muesli	25g
	Müller Fruit Corner—yoghurt	135g
	—fruit	40g
	Müller Honey Corner—yoghurt	135g
	—honey	40g
	St Ivel Shape twin pot—yoghurt	135g
	—fruit	35g
	Safeway Double Treat	175g
	Sainsburys Duet—yoghurt	135g
	—fruit	40g
	Sainsburys Duet Diet—yoghurt	115g
	—fruit	25g
	Ski Bio Split—yoghurt	135g
	—fruit	40g
	Tesco Fruit Plus Split	175g
	Tesco Healthy Eating Fruit Plus	140g
	Tesco Thick & Creamy	175g
Soya yoghurt	Granose	120g
Whipped yoghurt/Yoghurt mousse	Boots	100g

	Boots Shapers	*100g*
	Marks & Spencer Whisp (lightly whipped)	*125g*
	St Ivel Prize (lightly whipped) pack of 4, each	*90g*
	St Ivel Prize (lightly whipped) singles	*112g*

| **Yoghurt and cream desserts** | Boots Delights | *130g* |
| | Heinz yoghurt dessert for babies (jar) | *150g* |

Yoghurt drinks	Boots drinking yoghurt	*200g*
	Ski Cool (750 ml)	*795g*
	Ski Cool (200 ml)	*212g*
	Yop, large	*700g*
	Yop, standard	*200g*

Fromage Frais

	1 tablespoon	*45g*

Fromage frais is generally purchased in cartons of 60g or 100g. Examples of some common brands in each category are listed below:

60g pots

Chambourcy, with fruit purée
Danone Petit Gervais chocolate
Marks & Spencer, creamy with fruit pieces
Petits Filous—small
Safeway—small
Safeway, very low fat
Sainsburys, petit with fruit pieces
Somerfield, low fat
Thunderbirds

100g pots

Marks & Spencer, creamy with fruit purée
Petit Danone—large
Petits Filous—large
St Ivel Shape, virtually fat free
Safeway—large

Sainsburys, creamy with fruit
Sainsburys, very low fat, diet
Sainsburys, virtually fat free with fruit
    pieces
Tesco
Yoplait, fruit on the bottom
Yoplait light fruit

Other fromage frais	Country Love, fruit	*150g*
	Hippo Tots	*50g*
	Marks & Spencer Coco the Clown	*42g*
	Munch Bunch Pot Shots	*42g*
	Onken	*200g*
	Petit Danone—small	*50g*
	St Ivel Fiendish Faces	*50g*
Baby fromage frais	Baby Danone	*60g*
	Heinz (jar)	*163g*

Printed in the United Kingdom for The Stationery Office
J002364637 C6 11/10